A LIFE WITH PURPOSE

A LIFE WITH PURPOSE

REVEREND RICK WARREN
The Most Inspiring Pastor of Our Time

GEORGE MAIR

BERKLEY BOOKS, NEW YORK

THE BERKLEY PUBLISHING GROUP
Published by the Penguin Group
Penguin Group (USA) Inc.
375 Hudson Street, New York, New York 10014, USA
Penguin Group (Canada), 10 Alcorn Avenue, Toronto, Ontario M4V 3B2, Canada
(a division of Pearson Penguin Canada Inc.)
Penguin Books Ltd., 80 Strand, London WC2R 0RL, England
Penguin Group Ireland, 25 St. Stephen's Green, Dublin 2, Ireland (a division of Penguin Books Ltd.)
Penguin Group (Australia), 250 Camberwell Road, Camberwell, Victoria 3124, Australia
(a division of Pearson Australia Group Pty. Ltd.)
Penguin Books India Pvt. Ltd., 11 Community Centre, Panchsheel Park, New Delhi—110 017, India
Penguin Group (NZ), cnr. Airborne and Rosedale Roads, Albany, Auckland 1310, New Zealand
(a division of Pearson New Zealand Ltd.)
Penguin Books (South Africa) (Pty.) Ltd., 24 Sturdee Avenue, Rosebank, Johannesburg 2196, South Africa

Penguin Books Ltd., Registered Offices: 80 Strand, London WC2R 0RL, England

A LIFE WITH PURPOSE

This book is an original publication of The Berkley Publishing Group.

Unless otherwise noted, Scripture quotations are from the King James Version of the Bible.

Scripture quotations marked NLT are taken from the *Holy Bible,* New Living Translation, copyright © 1996. Used by permission of Tyndale House Publishers, Inc., Wheaton, IL 60189. All rights reserved.

Scripture quotations marked Msg. are taken from The Message, copyright © 1993, 1994, 1995, 1996, 2000, 2001, 2002. Used by permission of NavPress Publishing Group. All rights reserved.

First edition: March 2005

Berkley hardcover ISBN: 0-425-20174-0

This book has been catalogued with the Library of Congress.

PRINTED IN THE UNITED STATES OF AMERICA

10 9 8 7 6 5 4 3 2 1

CONTENTS

A LIFE WITH PURPOSE

INTRODUCTION

I 'LL never forget the first time I visited Rick Warren's Saddleback Church. I remember pulling onto Interstate 5 from my beach-town home in Dana Point. I was on my way to see a religious legend. Heading north on I-5, it struck me that there were several famous preachers in this area of South Orange County, California. Chuck Smith, Jr., son of legendary pastor Chuck Smith, presided at a converted bowling alley, now Capo Beach Calvary Church, which I attended with some regularity. Another evangelical TV preacher, Benny Hinn, lived in a $2 million waterfront home overlooking the Pacific Ocean near here. Robert Schuller was a little farther north of Saddleback up Interstate 5.

Schuller became famous from preaching on the roof of a

drive-in movie snack bar in the community of Garden Grove, near Disneyland. He would, in time, build one of the most dramatic churches in America, the Crystal Cathedral. He would also help many successful ministers, including the one I was now on my way to hear preach.

A few minutes' drive brought me to the El Toro Road exit. I turned east, unsure of where I was going. All I knew was that I was heading in the right general direction. I was excited about experiencing this unusual minister, whom my friends had urged me to see. They told me he was the most influential Protestant pastor in America. They also told me that if I just turned off onto El Toro Road I would easily find his Saddleback Church.

Heading toward the mountains on El Toro, past a shopping mall and giant retail outlets, the commercial stores thinned out and were replaced by apartment buildings, a retirement home and small convenience stores. The area was less developed, but road traffic was increasing. A moment later, I found myself in forested territory as the road slanted upward toward the rising Saddleback Mountains. All of a sudden, on a hilltop on my left, I saw a multistoried, beige, rectangular building. Traffic ahead of me was slowing to a stop, and there were orange-vested traffic control monitors directing us. I knew I must be in the right place because the next crossroad was labeled "Saddleback Church Road."

I crossed an overpass leading off El Toro Road onto Saddleback Road, and suddenly I was part of a stream of cars and SUVs being directed into a huge parking lot. I simply followed along, and parked right in front of the Worship Center—where all the spots were marked "Reserved for First-Time Guests." I got out and joined a mass of casually dressed people streaming toward a huge building that looked like a sports arena. It was surrounded by meticulous landscaping, steps, shaded walkways and water fountains. The crowd was in the forty-to-fifty age range, with a mixture of teen children and young couples pushing strollers.

The landscaping was pure California—sycamores, Monterey pines, jacarandas blooming soft blue in the summer, spreading bougainvilleas in scarlet and purple, yellow daylilies, old-fashioned roses here and there, grasses and other ground cover, wild irises and geraniums. Stately old palm trees stood guard near the main entrance to the Worship Center, shading benches for worshipers. I later found out that a sound system carried the services throughout the complex, so overflow crowds or those who simply prefer to sit outside could enjoy the sermon and music in chairs set out under the shade trees. I took a path around one side of the center that led to a walkway cantilevered over a small ravine. The spectacular view below was a deftly lighted forest of trees on one side and on the other an amphitheater.

I looked for a cross, or other signs of a Christian center, and finally spied a slender cross of dark metal above the complex—more a piece of art than a religious symbol. There were maps on easels posted around, showing the various facilities of the complex: the Worship Center with its two green rooms, the Children's Center with nursery and playground, the education building, two huge tents, the café, offices, and several huge parking lots. Water gushed continually over stones into the roughly triangular decorative baptismal pool; a curving row of steps along one side led the participants into the water for the ritual. It didn't look like a baptismal font, just an eye-catching ingredient in the landscape.

The Worship Center dominated the area. Two sides of it were ground-to-roof glass, which reflected the greenery around them and made the building a part of the natural surroundings. These walls marked Saddleback with a contemporary stamp, but the neutral stucco and stone arch work in other walls of the building had an almost Biblical feel. Etched into the glass above the wide double doors leading inside were significant phrases. I would learn later they were from the pastor's best-selling book about forty days of purpose.

Surrounding the Worship Center was a large courtyard, which was spotted with industrial-looking covered stands. On those stands was literature on the various free classes and studies offered by the church—helpful information about groups keyed to individual problems such as addiction, divorce, depression and child rearing. Smiling church members were milling about, offering cheerful greetings to all.

As I walked up the steps toward the giant building, a smiling man stepped forward, extended his hand and greeted me with "Good Morning. We're happy you can be with us this morning." I returned the greeting and thought to myself, "I've been going to church for fifty years and that's the first time anyone has welcomed me so cordially." I wasn't even inside and already felt welcome. Easy parking, a welcoming handshake and smile. We were off to a good start!

As I entered the huge rectangular meeting hall, I looked around. It was unlike any other church I had ever seen. It had a high ceiling with concrete flooring, and row after row of seats stretching up high in the back. I would later learn it held thirty-two hundred seats. In front was a big stage accommodating a chorus, a band, and the pulpit. Banks of lights provided strategic illumination of the various elements. Suspended from the ceiling was an array of electronics including five giant TV screens. Everyone in the hall would be able to easily see and hear the sermon.

In many ways, the meeting hall was more like a basketball stadium than a church—there were almost no Christian symbols or artifacts in view. I knew there had to be a

Christian cross somewhere inside, but I couldn't find it. I didn't know it then, but the lack of Christian imagery was characteristic of the new wave of so-called mega churches in America.

I found a seat—not a bench or a pew, but a separate plastic and metal seat that could, if needed, be detached from its adjoining seats. I sat down and enjoyed the upbeat pop music being played by the band and chorus. Then I turned to the program and had another surprise: there was a "quiz" to help us follow the pastor's message. The subject of the sermon was "God's Passion for You." The quiz started with a reference to the Bible (based on John 3:16) about "God's _____ (fill in the blank: *love*) for humanity" and continued through the sermon. It was going to be fascinating following the preacher as if I were in class with a teacher.

Then, my attention suddenly shifted to the altar stage as the music changed tempo and the stage lights came on. A stocky middle-aged man with thinning hair and glasses appeared, wearing sneakers with no socks and a Hawaiian shirt. He looked like he was part of the sound crew coming on to adjust the microphone in preparation for the minister and his sermon.

The auditorium became silent and the man from the sound crew began to speak. Oh, my gosh! The "sound technician" *was* the pastor. Here was the most admired Protestant preacher in America looking like my cousin Walter getting ready to start the barbecue. It stunned me.

He went into his message with such enthusiasm it was hard not to pay attention as he took us step by step through the lesson from John. Then, suddenly, after about fifteen minutes, he stopped talking, took his Bible and walked off stage. We were treated to an upbeat Christian song by the band, and then another minister appeared and took the first man's place as if on cue. He also spoke for fifteen minutes and then went off stage. Following another musical interlude, another speaker appeared. This repeated twice more and then the service was over. Thousands of people—all happy and smiling—moved outside and mingled in the tailored grounds of the Saddleback Church.

I had just experienced Rick Warren, who is considered by many to be America's most important Protestant religious leader. I was impressed by his sermon and presentation—even if I wasn't quite adjusted to his fifteen-minute sermon style. As I walked out, I thought about what I had known about him before coming here this sunny Sunday morning. The central fact was that this man, who had never had a church before, had come to this community a little over twenty years ago with no money, no ministry, no experience running a church, no place to live, a wife who wasn't sure she should have married him, and a new baby. With determination and faith, he had created one of the biggest and most powerful Christian churches in America.

His ministry, and his Purpose-Driven philosophy, is devoted to helping people find their purpose on Earth, and to teaching Christian churches how to expand through evangelism. Some religious scholars and ministers recoil at Warren's pragmatic approach to church expansion, which on the surface seems more corporate than spiritual. It is true he has created a multimillion-dollar nonprofit enterprise in which he applies business sense to religious challenges. But the reality is also that it has inspired thousands of other ministers, who regard him as a spiritual superman.

His recent book, *The Purpose-Driven Life: What on Earth Am I Here For?* which has sold millions of copies in twelve languages, stands as a measure of that success. This book lays out a forty-day plan to discover God's purpose for one's life. Its first sentence—"It's not about you"—sets the tone, putting it at odds with self-help groups and preachers who focus on personal happiness. It is colloquially referred to as "Rick's anti self-help book."

I knew one thing for sure about Rick Warren: his is a fascinating story. A humble man with humble beginnings, he is changing America—and the world—"one soul at a time." Yet, for all his achievements, Warren is not a celebrity. That's not how he sees himself. He takes pains to maintain his low profile. He practices what he preaches: it's not about him. He rarely gives interviews, and won't be found in front of a television camera making speeches on the steps of City Hall. His focus is on his ministry and fulfilling his calling to help churches and individuals remember that our purpose is to fulfill God's purpose.

After hearing him preach and experiencing Saddleback Church, I understand why millions are listening to this man, and knew that the story behind the movement deserves to be told. This is my attempt to tell that story.

In researching this book, I've been able to speak with friends and family of Rick Warren and have been able to glean insight into who the man is, and how he came to the place he is today. I find his story fascinating and inspiring, and I offer it to you so that you, too, can understand and learn from this man who lives his life with such purpose.

CHAPTER ONE

THE CHURCH IN AMERICA

NO one can deny that Rick Warren and his Saddle-back Church are true religious phenomena. But the roots of Warren's faith—in fact, the roots of almost every religion in the United States today—extend far into the past. These roots are older than America itself. In order to truly understand Rick Warren's Saddleback ministry, and its place in the scope of Christianity, in the country and in the world, we must first take a quick look at the history of religion in America.

American Religion: A Brief History

From the very beginning, religion played a pivotal role in the settlement of the New World. The earliest settlers, who started to arrive in the 1600s, were groups of Europeans trying to escape religious persecution from government officials and other religious groups. The first group to move en masse to the New World was the English Separatists, more commonly known as the Pilgrims. The Separatists believed the Church of England was doomed and wanted to leave it behind. After a short-lived attempt to move to Holland, they relocated to the area that would become known as Massachusetts.

In 1629, the Puritans asked for a license to start the Massachusetts Bay Company and were granted permission from the King of England, Charles I. Lead by John Winthrop, they started arriving in Massachusetts in 1630. By 1642, twenty thousand Puritans had made the journey across the Atlantic in what is known as the Great Migration.

From the start, America was a land of religious freedom. New settlers were not only able to escape the religious pressures of Europe, but also granted the liberty to expand and evolve in ways they couldn't have back home. The Puritans are a prime example of that fact. As their numbers grew, different groups began disagreeing with one another. Thomas Hooker led a group to Connecticut in 1636 and Roger Williams led another group to Rhode Island in 1644. Each cell put down its own roots and flourished.

The open geography of the New World made it possible for these kinds of splinter groups to form and move away from one another. This is a significant fact: we are all too aware that limited land geographies, like the modern Middle East, do not bode well for religious freedom. But with unlimited land and opportunity in America, religious groups knew neither physical nor spiritual boundaries.

Not all American religions were children of existing faiths: some entirely new religions were started in the New World. Joseph Smith started Mormonism in 1832 in New York. His followers, who practiced polygamy, were persecuted and forced to move to Nauvoo, Illinois. There, Smith destroyed a printing press that published a newspaper criticizing him and was arrested; while he was in jail, a mob broke in and killed him. Brigham Young became the new Mormon leader and led the group out to Salt Lake City in what is now Utah. The Mormons are perhaps the best example of how the sheer size of the American landscape allowed new religions to flourish.

Of course, land is a fixed commodity. Even in the United States, with its seemingly endless natural resources, religious groups were eventually forced to coexist. But even as the population grew and land became less plentiful, other fundamental American institutions took over the role that sheer space had once played. One was the chosen form of government: democracy. People voted privately for their political leaders—there was no chance of being persecuted on the basis of political affiliation. Furthermore, no religion was officially tied to any one political party. The government wrote into law that America would always protect religious freedom.

The second factor that provided for religious growth was economic. America was a predominantly free-market economy built by entrepreneurs. The ability to create products and services was a natural result of the free-enterprise system; so was the ability to adapt business strategies to better cater to changing markets. In the twentieth century, some religious leaders figured this out. They became known as New Age ministers, and were the first ones to gear religion towards the masses of unaffiliated members of the population.

These factors created a fertile breeding ground for religion in America, and fueled an increase in the number of churches and synagogues in the country during the 1920s. Meanwhile, existing religious denominations continued to evolve and adapt. Protestants experienced a divide between modern thinkers, who identified with modern Bible critics, and fundamental thinkers, who followed the Bible literally. More immigrants from entirely different European communities continued to pour into the country, particularly inflating the numbers of the Roman Catholic and Jewish congregations. The religious melting pot kept on growing, mixing, and diversifying.

Religion in America grew until the 1960s, when radical changes occurred. The sixties generation openly revolted against everything that represented the past and the establishment. Parents, elders—authority of any kind—were violently challenged. Drugs and sex were not only rampant, but publicly displayed. At the center of everything considered authoritarian and "old" was religion. Church attendance by the baby boomer youth population plummeted in the 1960s.

Gradually, as the boomers aged through the seventies and into the eighties, they changed their attitudes. They got married. They had children, and suddenly were responsible for someone other than themselves. The old issues of drugs, sex, and personal conflict arose again, only this time the Boomers were the parents facing rebellion from their children. This change, as well as other social and political trends, resulted in a reinvigoration of the search for God.

Religion in America Today

Present-day America is without a doubt one of the most religiously diverse countries in the world. There are approximately two thousand different religions currently in the United States, ranging from Muslim to Christian to New Age to Zoroastrian. Approximately 30 percent of the population call themselves Evangelical Protestants, which makes them the biggest religious group in the country. The Protestants encompass several large denominations, including the Southern Baptist, Methodist, and Pentecostal.

The main lesson of Protestantism centers on the concept that a person should follow the Bible and live an honest life embracing God and Jesus. As a result of his or her faith, a person will be rewarded with a life of happiness and satisfaction. American Protestantism has undergone several schisms and transformations since the original Europeans first landed. But in the twentieth century, two preachers stand out: the Reverend Robert Schuller and the Reverend Billy Graham.

The efforts of Graham and Schuller and many others combined to create a phenomenon known as the Church Growth Movement. The most recognizable product of this movement is the mega-church. These gigantic churches have anywhere from two thousand to twenty thousand worshipers. They consciously avoid the dress-up-on-Sunday and listen-to-the-preacher-drone type of Christian church experience. Instead, mega-churches have multimedia presentations coupled with live entertainment that keep the service moving, the message flowing, and the congregation's attention piqued.

Mega-church pastors don't just want you to come in, listen to the sermon, drop change in the box, and leave. They want you to show up early for meetings, linger after for some coffee, and stop by during the week to play some soccer. The true mega-church experience isn't a one-hour-a-week gathering. These churches are designed to get you to come back for more community interaction, more activity, and more of the Word. Mega-churches engage the congregation and get the congregation engaged in the church. They provide a mutually beneficial relationship.

How do mega-churches grow? Why do people attend them in droves? Before we answer that, we have to ask another question: where did these people go to church before? For many of them, the answer is "nowhere." While 141 million Americans—roughly 50 percent of the population— say they belong to a church, approximately 85 million more say they believe in God but don't belong anywhere specific. These people are also known as "seekers." They believe in God, but haven't found the right Christian community that caters to their needs.

So, how do mega-churches go about attracting these large masses? Historically in America, businesses and other organizations grew by reproducing the same things very efficiently. As Henry Ford once famously said, "They can have their car any color they want as long as it's black." In the traditional church's case, however, this one-size-fits-all method is what inhibited its ability to grow.

Mega-churches realized that attracting large masses could only be achieved by catering to individuals' specific religious needs. They knew that the "seekers" or "unchurched" had been flying under the radar for many years by practicing a sort of mini-religion of their own through the use of yoga classes, meditation centers, and small Bible study groups. Their abhorrence of the old-fashioned ram-it-down-your-throat form of religion made them into a very large Christian market just waiting to be tapped.

How exactly does a mega-church get these seekers through the door? By expanding its offerings beyond Sunday services. By changing what Sunday service is, how it is delivered, and who delivers it. By creating small groups within the church that allow the worshiper to feel both a part of something special and a part of something bigger. But more than anything else, mega-churches owe their success to their ability to listen to what the unchurched want and deliver it. Mega-churches make themselves *significant* to the masses of seekers.

The Evolving Giant

On September 11, 2001, America, and American religion, changed. The Friday following September 11, President Bush called for a day of national prayer and asked all people to attend a noontime service. On that workday and school day, with no planned holiday or vacation, people attended church services throughout the country in numbers never seen before—not even at Christmas or Easter.

Everyone remembers that day and what it meant. No words. No socializing. No complaining about parking four blocks away and walking. No discussion about lunch. No errands to run. Simply a solemn procession to church, as people silently pondered what the world had come to. Praying for the victims and their families. Holding hands in community. Holding each other in support. Wondering what the future held for their children. Asking God for guidance.

September 11 gave pause to people caught up in their own lives, their own problems, and their own worlds. They stopped to wonder, "Is there something bigger here? Something much bigger than my little world? What can I do to help it survive?"

9/11 made people fearful in a way they had never been before. But it also led them to ask, "Where can I find the

Lord?" In that sense, 9/11 was the catalyst for bringing many men and women—particularly "seekers"—to fulfillment.

From that day forward, religion started to make inroads into popular culture in ways that is hadn't done for many years. Today we can see indicators of the growth and evolution of religion in America in almost every form of mass media. The popularity of Dan Brown's *The DaVinci Code*, a mystery novel with a religious theme, has certainly brought religion into mainstream reading material. Also fantastically popular are the *Left Behind* novels based on the Book of Revelations, which have sold more than 60 million copies. Mel Gibson's movie *The Passion* grossed over $100 million. Not to be outdone by the bookstores or the box office, an estimated 128 million Internet users say they have gone online to seek religious or spiritual guidance.

One website, Beliefnet.com, caters to 4 million people a day. The founder and editor of the site, Steven Waldman, said, "People are cobbling together their own personalized spiritual plans, rather than relying on clergy." This points back to the approach that attracts people to mega-churches: providing many small groups that cater to specific community needs and individual fulfillment, in the context of a greater whole. As much as the Internet can provide a vast array of choices for an individual, allowing him or her to remain in the comfort of home, the mega-church also offers

something the individual craves: the warmth of being accepted into a community.

Mega-churches have also been able to identify what
turns parishioners off. Americans do not go to church to be
forced into a crusade or to judge sinners. Going to church is
based on belief, not religious dogmatism. A 1965 Gallup
poll showed that 50 percent of the people surveyed said
they went to church so they could learn to live a better life,
and that the church was supposed to fulfill that need. They
wanted to live better day by day, not just to be lectured on
Sunday as though they were always wrong and sinful. Today,
the number of people who view churches as having the responsibility of teaching a better way of living has risen to almost 75 percent. This evidence suggests that fulfillment is
what the seeker wants. And fulfillment is what mega-
churches, like Rick Warren's Saddleback, are delivering.

As religion in America continues to grow and evolve, so
will its churches. Rick will keep trying to help more
churches achieve the success of Saddleback. He's already
well on his way: his Purpose-Driven Movement has already
started hundreds of churches in America. (We'll talk more
about Saddleback Church and the Purpose-Driven movement in chapters seven and eight). Additionally, he is on a
campaign to form hundreds of Protestant churches in Africa
and Latin America. His goal: to help the world discover
God and God's purpose for their lives.

*   *   *

From the earliest Puritan settlers to the most modern mega-church attendees, the threads of Christianity have been tightly woven with the threads of American culture. Rick Warren is a product of that culture. Now it's time to take a closer look at the people, choices, and events that made Rick into the pastor that he is today.

CHAPTER TWO

PLANTING THE SEEDS

A S it is with any successful person, influential people and events helped Rick Warren become the
man he is today. The primary influences on Rick's
life were his parents, Dot and Jimmy Warren, Sr. The elder
Warrens were raised in the southeastern United States and
were active in the southern Baptist Church. They set an example of Christian living for Rick to follow, and that example would eventually became the foundation for his
successful ministry at Saddleback.

Going to California to Do God's Work

In the early 1950s, Jimmy Sr. followed God's call to evangelize and moved to California. He was a pioneer—a pioneer for the Southern Baptist Church. Starting out at the Golden Gate Baptist Theological Seminary in Berkeley, Jimmy Sr. did whatever it took to help the seminary thrive. He did handiwork and helped out with other people's classes. It wasn't about the title or position for Jimmy Sr. He just wanted to do the Lord's work.

In 1958, the Golden Gate Baptist Theological Seminary moved from Berkeley to just north of the Golden Gate Bridge, in a community called Mill Valley. The Warrens were, of course, major factors in helping to orchestrate that move. Jimmy Sr. and Dot moved their family into Sausalito, right next to Mill Valley.

Jimmy Sr. worked in the Northern California area as a traveling pastor. He would travel as far away as Annapolis, a small lumber community about a hundred miles northwest of San Francisco. Battling the weather, the unpaved roads, and logging trucks appearing out of nowhere around hairpin turns, Jimmy Sr. voyaged to small, isolated communities to preach. He always reached out to those that would otherwise not have heard the teaching of Jesus Christ.

Although he had to drive through fog over winding mountain roads, which were mostly mud in the wintertime, Jimmy Sr. was more reliable than the local postman. Many of his journeys to outlying parishes in Sonoma County were a full half-day ride by car one way. But if it was to help one parish, one family, or one person hear the Word of God, Jimmy Sr. was ready to do God's work delivering it.

As a traveling pastor to local parishes, he became well known in the Sonoma County and San Francisco area. The California Southern Baptist Convention also noticed his work. In 1964, they appointed Jimmy Warren, Sr., the director of missions for the Yokayo Association. Basically, this meant that Jimmy Sr. was the pastor to the other pastors: he was in charge of helping the local pastors with their churches. In that sense, Jimmy Sr.'s work for God was expanding His operations in the area.

After getting this new position in the church, Jimmy Warren, Sr., and his family moved farther north to a more central location in the Redwood Valley of Mendocino County. Their house was located about seven miles north of Ukiah, the Mendocino County seat. This is where Rick, his brother, Jimmy Jr., and his sister, Chaundel, would grow up during their most influential years, their teens.

Mendocino County was very remote and covered two thousand square miles of rugged Northern California coast and inland valleys. In the sixties there weren't many people living there—sixty thousand total, with twelve thousand in or around Ukiah. There seemed to be more cows and sheep per square mile than people. But there were a couple of major industries that managed to thrive in the area: the lumber and grape-growing businesses. Vineyard grapes were just about the only crop that could grow in the soil of Mendocino County. At first, grape vineyards were few and far between, but as California wine became more popular in the sixties, grape production increased.

Ukiah had several sawmills, and the smell of cut lumber permeated the area. As the construction boom of the sixties continued to roar, masonite's popularity expanded. The masonite plant in town took the wood chips from the sawmills and made fiberboard. Logging trucks would bring trees in to the mills, and railroad freight cars would take the cut lumber south to the construction-crazed communities growing down there. The 101 Freeway was expanded to four lanes in the Ukiah area to handle the increased traffic load.

In Ukiah, lumberjacks and millwrights had steady work and a good place to raise a family. The beauty of that kind of rural environment was that it forced people to be self-reliant—there were no convenience stores on the corner. But at the same time, people were willing to lend a helping hand when neighbors needed it. This forged self-respect as well as mutual respect in the community. It bonded the neighbors to one another. Ukiah offered open spaces, a helpful community, a new high school, and the opportunity to raise a family in the church through the work of Jimmy Warren, Sr., and his family. What could be better for the people of the Redwood Valley in the 1960s?

The Turbulent Sixties

In the 1960s, the world was changing, and changing rapidly. Television was in many households, and people could see live reports of news events. Vietnam was the hot-button issue of the generation. Eighteen year-olds were being drafted and sent off to an undeclared war. Many were dying and many more were coming home wounded. College campuses were exploding in protest, violence, and bloodshed. This open challenge—people questioning America's commitment to the War—led to everything being challenged. There were the assassinations of John F. Kennedy, Dr. Martin Luther King, Jr., and Robert Kennedy. Race riots burned cities, including Chicago, Detroit, Los Angeles, and Memphis. The Civil Rights Movement was working to create a land of opportunity for minorities. Even bras were being burned. The "Now" Generation was coming of age with cars, McDonald's, TV news, drive-in theaters, and drugs. Its members became accustomed to demanding instant gratification of the urge to travel, and to see world events. Life was simultaneously accelerating and becoming more complex and stressful.

American society was in total upheaval. How kids dressed, how they wore their hair, and how they took care of themselves changed. How they spoke to the older generation—their parents, their teachers, civil authorities, or anyone else that represented the past—changed. And the change had a challenging, disrespectful tone. It was "hip" to be antiwar, antiestablishment, and anti-parent. Teenagers openly disobeyed their parents and disdained what they stood for. Drug use was rampant, both as an "escape" from the pressures of the world and a new way to get "high" on life. The teachings of drug guru Timothy Leary spread in influence. The advent of the birth control pill created a sexual revolution, challenging traditional values. Sexually transmitted diseases began to spread rampantly. The Beatles appeared on *The Ed Sullivan Show,* their long hair sending teenage girls into a frenzy and parents into shocking disapproval. Teenage boys noticed both reactions, and some immediately began to grow their hair long.

The heart of this countercultural movement was split between two districts, both just south of Ukiah. One was Berkeley, where Jimmy Warren, Sr., had begun his California ministry. The University of California at Berkeley became the center of student cultural unrest. The second district was Haight-Ashbury. "The Haight," as it was called, in San Francisco was where people went when they dropped out of society and dropped into something different: the drug culture.

It was during the sixties that Charles Manson and his family paid a visit to the Redwood Valley. And Jim Jones started a new church movement when he opened his People's Temple in the area preaching his apocalyptic cult message. It was a time of emotional and spiritual chaos for many people, and they were turning anywhere but Jesus Christ to get their answers.

Riding Out the Tide

The headlines of the sixties were sex, drugs, war, and a searing generation gap that was disrupting the traditional family. The younger generation was engaged in a confrontation with their parents, and everything their parents believed in: honor to country, honor to community, honor to family, respecting one's elders, and believing in God. Right in the middle of the schism stood the biggest symbol of the parental establishment: the church.

Rick Warren was certainly a product of that turbulent generation. But he managed to find ways to adapt to the 1960s while maintaining his strong belief in the Lord. He understood that what someone wore and how he wore it played a big role in how others responded to the person. So he grew his hair long and played guitar while attending Ukiah High School. But he wasn't trying to make a statement. Those were his ways of making himself seem more approachable, like he was "one of the guys," so he could get his peers to listen to the teachings of the Lord. By dressing as a "local," as he still does today, preaching his sermons in a Hawaiian shirt and sandals at Saddleback Community Church, he earned people's confidence. In turn they lent him an open ear to what he had to say about Jesus Christ. And they were people who desperately needed to know they had a choice in their life other than drugs, violence, and parent-bashing. The other choice was to follow Jesus.

Rick started following in his parents' evangelical footsteps while he was still a high school student. In his time at Ukiah High School (1968 to 1971), he started a Christian Youth movement. He created the first Christian club on campus: The Fishers of Men Club. Through his talent as a guitar player, he produced a Christian musical and sponsored after-school rock concerts. Using his ability to deliver the Word of the Lord in written form, he developed and distributed a Christian newspaper. Today at Saddleback he is still using music and the written word through his successful books, his newsletter, and his website, to spread the Word of Jesus Christ.

The Warrens helped save countless young people who

were caught up in the confusion and chaos of the sixties. Between Jimmy Warren, Sr.'s youth ministry movement (which we'll hear more about later in this chapter) and Rick Warren's ministry for youth at Ukiah High School, teenagers were given a choice to do something other than drugs or running away to Haight-Ashbury to avoid life's challenges. They could choose to meet life head-on with the aid of Jesus.

Garry Zeek is one person who heard that message. Four years younger than Rick Warren, Garry graduated from Ukiah High School in 1975. While he was still in school, he and a few of his Ukiah High friends went out drinking. As the liquor got the best of their better judgment, they decided to do something bold. They decided to go pay a visit to Jim Jones's People's Temple in Redwood Valley.

After weaving and bobbing along the highway out of town, they turned at the entry to the People's Temple and drove in. They went looking for trouble, and they found it. After they entered the compound, guards carrying automatic weapons surrounded the car. Forced outside, the drunken, rowdy teenagers were suddenly sober, quiet, and very scared. The only thing that saved them was the fact that Garry Zeek knew one of Jim Jones's sons. Jones's son came out, vouched for Garry, and the scared-straight teenagers were let go.

That close call put Garry Zeek on the path to the Lord.

He joined the Fishers of Men Club originally started by Rick Warren. Although Rick had already graduated several years before, the effect of what he had done was still rippling out to the youth community. By the time Garry Zeek joined the club, it had grown from a small group to a regular gathering, and new members were constantly joining.

Saving people and doing God's work—that's what Jimmy Warren, Sr., and Rick Warren were doing in Ukiah in the 1960s. Whether is was simply by giving people the opportunity to gather as a community (which is what missions are all about) or by bringing about a full-blown conversion, like the one Garry Zeek had, the father and son were evangelizing. In Garry's case, the church offered him a place to turn after he got a serious wake-up call.

It seems ironic that the sixties, the era that fundamentally challenged established religion in America, would have been such an important time for Rick Warren's growth as a minister. But it was. It was during that time that Rick developed his high school ministry. In retrospect, we can now understand that the sixties created an entire generation of unchurched men and women who would later become the very people Rick would target for his Saddleback Valley Community Church. The fact that Rick Warren's ministry exists today in large part because of the 1960s is a twist that could only be inspired by the Lord.

Growing Churches and Church Leaders

Through those trying times, Jimmy Warren, Sr., like his son, faced an incredibly difficult task. And also like his son, despite the pressures and challenges of the times, he was able to persevere, never giving up on his mission of establishing, developing, growing, and working with the numerous small missions in the Mendocino County area.

Jimmy Sr. realized that he, too, had to focus on young men and women. They were wandering both physically and in spirit—he knew he needed to provide them with a beacon to find their way home. To accomplish this task, he located and hired youth pastors. He was the first director of missions in the area to do so.

Jimmy also realized that Christian youths felt isolated in their small community parishes. He fostered youth programs that included all of the churches in the Yokayo Association (the Mendocino County area parishes). Moving events from church to church gave people a sense of what the rest of the community was like, while giving each parish a sense of being the root system for that particular youth event. He created a feeling of largeness out of a small cluster of churches, a successful approach that his son Rick would take in later years at Saddleback.

In addition to his youth program, Jimmy Sr. also focused on continuing to grow the church. He had an entrepreneurial approach to church building. He recognized that his strength was to build new churches, but also that it was someone else's job to run them after he constructed them. That's why he was continually involved in reaching out to new communities, creating new churches, and bringing new people into the church. Rick Warren would later incorporate a similar entrepreneurial attitude at the Saddleback Valley Community Church. The son's approach would be slightly different, but it would provide the same effect as his father's had.

Jimmy Sr. helped start at least three churches in the Mendocino area, one of which was in the Redwood Valley. In January 1972, the first service was held in the living room of the Warren home. Soon the congregation expanded, and the services were moved to a larger room upstairs. But the growth didn't stop. As the congregation doubled and tripled in number, the church had to find larger accommodations. They moved to the largest facility they could find to host fifty worshipers for Easter service: the old milk barn near the Warrens' house. Finally, on July 9, 1972, the mission was officially organized as the First Baptist Church of Redwood Valley. The following February (1973), the congregation broke ground for its own facility, less than two hundred yards from the Warrens' home. The first service there was appropriately held on Easter of that year.

In years to come, Rick Warren would grow his congregation in a similar fashion, only he would move to seventy nine different places before settling in at the current Saddleback location. By the time he settled, Rick had a few more parishioners to accommodate than the folks at Redwood Valley: ten thousand.

The Warren Legacy

Jimmy Warren, Sr.'s success was not just measured in the physical churches he created; it was also measured in the number of leaders he created through his ministry, especially his youth ministry, who helped grow the Baptist Church. These leaders not only helped in the Yokayo Association, but also spread the Word around the world. During Jimmy Warren's ministry, there were at least twenty-five noted members of the Yokayo Association youth ministry programs who became successful pastors within the Baptist Church. Here is one such story.

Joe Fry became the pastor of the Trinity Baptist Church of Ukiah during the 1960s, when Jimmy Warren, Sr., was the director of missions in the area. He says that Jimmy Sr. "more or less adopted me when I came to Ukiah." Joe had never been there before, but he knew he was to serve the Lord in his mission at Trinity. He says now that the Warrens made his mission so much easier to accomplish. Jimmy Warren, Sr., and Dot made sure Joe didn't have to worry about starting a congregation, building or maintaining a church, or most important, feeling welcomed by the community as the new pastor. They took care of all of those things themselves.

Today, Joe probably understands more than ever what the Warrens meant to him and his ministry at Trinity. Joe is the pastor of the newly formed Crossroads Church in Ukiah. Just as the Warrens did when they started their ministry in the Ukiah area some forty years earlier, Joe Fry had to start out small. He started with less than ten people in his congregation. In two years, it's grown to over two hundred parishioners. In typical mission fashion, the church started out in a house and moved several times. Now the congregation meets at the Ukiah Convention Center, which used to be a JC Penney store. Joe Fry and his congregation are currently looking for a permanent home for Crossroads Church.

It's obvious that Rick Warren watched his father foster other pastors and took that example to heart. Today his ministry focuses more on developing new leaders than anything else. Watching his father help the likes of Joe Fry succeed at Trinity set the example that Rick would follow. He learned that if he helped develop leaders quickly by removing some of the obstacles he and his father had to go through, the church could grow faster and its pastors could focus more on evangelizing. (We'll talk more about the details of how Rick Warren makes this work in later chapters.)

Jimmy Sr. would be the first to tell you his success was not his own. He'd just say he was doing the Lord's will, and working for the Lord. Then he'd tell you how many people helped with his mission. But it all started right there in the Warren household. While Jimmy was going out to people's houses to help build the church community, Dot was opening the Warren house to those seeking help.

Rick Warren grew up around strangers. But the truth was, in the Warren household, strangers were never treated as outsiders. Even when people came into the Warren home for the first time, Dot made them feel like they had been visiting for years and were old friends of the family. This true feeling of openness, of welcoming people and making them feel comfortable, is evident today at Rick Warren's Saddleback Valley Community Church. Newcomers get the preferred parking spots and are welcomed warmly by the church greeters as they enter Saddleback.

Those kinds of stories make it easy to call Jimmy Warren, Sr.'s ministry a success. He set an example that many pastors, including his own son, would follow, and tirelessly did the Lord's work all his life. It isn't just the church buildings he helped open that remain as his legacy—it's the many leaders he influenced who further spread the Word of God.

Building Blocks of Greatness

Rick Warren had a strong foundation on which to build his successful ministry: his parents gave him everything he needed to achieve all he could in the name of the Lord. Jimmy Sr. and Dot truly were a great team. Jimmy did every-thing he could to help build churches. He was a contractor, maintenance repairman, and pastor. He was always helping people, whether it was by tinkering with their own homes or their spiritual beings. Jimmy Sr. did God's work with his hands, his heart, and his soul. Everybody in the communi-ties he touched noticed his kind spirit and good nature.

If Jimmy Sr. was the physical energy of God's work in the Warren household, Dot was the warm hearth. No one was a stranger to Dot, and all were welcome in the Warren kitchen. She wasn't just a pastor's wife, either—she knew the Bible and understood the Word of the Lord. Visiting pastors who knew Dot Warren used to think it was a subtle compliment if, when they were preaching, Dot nodded her head as if she had heard a new message.

This combination—the energy and work ethic of Jimmy

Sr. and the benevolence of Dot—is what made Rick Warren into the immensely successful pastor he is today. Rick's
constant desire to get things done in his father's spirit of
persistence is what helped drive him to create the Saddleback Church. He learned that no challenge can withstand
the constant pressure of effort. But Rick also adheres to his
mother's example: that no one is a stranger. That's what
drives Rick to seek, find, invite, and convert people to the
Word of Jesus Christ. Everyone is welcome at Rick's Saddleback Church.

The elder Warrens remained in the Northern California
area after they retired, moving to the Sierra foothill community of Pioneer. Dot passed of a heart attack in her
kitchen while preparing a lunch for some guests. Her
warmth and generosity were ever-present, right up to the
moment she died.

Instead of a funeral memorial, the Warren family decided to have a Celebration of Life for Dot. The focus was
on what Dot gave to the community, to the church, and to
everyone who came into her kitchen as a welcomed guest.
At the celebration, Rick delivered a heartfelt reflection on
his mother's life. There was an overflow crowd paying its re-
spects to a woman who always opened her household. Since
not everyone could see or hear the service, an impromptu
television setup was arranged. There was a camera inside

the church, and a large monitor placed outside for everyone to see and hear. A side note of humor in the service was one of Rick's comments. He had promised his mom that he would never turn into one of "those TV evangelists." During the service, he stopped and wondered if he could continue. He pointed out the camera and his image on a large screen outside, and wondered whether or not he was sticking to his vow to his mother. That brought a round of laughter from the gathering.

After Dot passed, Jimmy Warren, Sr., moved to Southern California to be near Rick and Rick's sister, Chaundel, who worked for him at Saddleback. Jimmy Sr. eventually succumbed to cancer. Even on his deathbed, he talked about "saving one more for Jesus." That passion is still what drives Rick today. Like his father, he is doing the Lord's work to save one more.

There were other family members who influenced Rick, as well. Chaundel and her husband, Tom Holladay, were significant contributors to the Trinity Baptist Church growth. Chaundel was Joe Fry's secretary at Trinity and Tom was Joe's associate pastor. Tom and Chaundel were a good team because they balanced each other out. Chaundel was an energetic, outgoing, hard-charging woman with a get-things-done attitude. Tom was steady and laid back in his approach. Rick Warren's ministry in many ways reflects a combination of Chaundel's energy and endless effort, and

Tom's softer style. But nothing could quite come close to the effect his mother and father had.

Rick Warren derives his success today from combining all the best elements of the people who influenced him growing up. Jimmy Sr., in particular, set the example of a life dedicated God's work, which Rick would so ardently follow years later. The seeds for Rick's Saddleback ministry had been planted at Ukiah High School, and were already starting to sprout. But he still had a long way to go before he could think about staring his own church. So, after graduating from Ukiah in 1971, Rick turned his preparation for ministry to a more formal approach.

CHAPTER THREE

PREPARING FOR MINISTRY

R ICK Warren graduated from Ukiah High School in 1971 as president of his class. Soon after, he married his high school sweetheart, Kay, whom he met when he was sixteen. Rick was doing a rather energetic impersonation of Billy Graham in a church talent contest. Kay was not at all impressed with Rick's talent or his outward attitude —he was a bit too flamboyant for her. But, as is the case often in Rick's life, what appears to be on the outside is not necessarily what's true on the inside. He is, at times, a contradiction in terms. But we shall see throughout this chapter and the following chapters that the contradictions are only based on people see on the surface, not the true Rick Warren they learn to love.

Kay is a prime example: she initially misjudged the man she grew to know, date, love, marry, and raise a family with. Underneath it all, the brash young man Kay first experienced was really the kind, God-serving man she'd always wanted to marry—the man she would eventually join in a quest for his own ministry. On the day they met, he was as bold-acting as Billy Graham, but in reality he's unpretentious in his day-to-day mannerisms. He isn't politically outspoken, but he has powerful ideas and preaches to one of the largest churches in the country. He wants to convert the many, but he does so by focusing on the few. But through all of the apparent contradictions, one thing is certain: Rick Warren has always lived to serve Jesus.

California Baptist University

After high school, Rick applied to the only Baptist university on the West Coast, California Baptist in Riverside, and was accepted. Founded in 1955, California Baptist University sits on fifty-two acres of land, eighty miles east of Los Angeles. Built in the typical California mission style—beige stucco walls with a red tile roof—it offers curriculums in liberal arts, science, psychology, and education, and of course has a strong biblical studies program. The school emphasizes "biblical integration"—connecting the Bible to all majors offered and hiring faculty members who exemplify passion for both Christ and learning.

Rick got involved in the Baptist youth community at California Baptist. Title IX had been passed in 1973, and the result was more people getting involved in youth sports and fitness. Rick felt that a weight-lifting facility would be a great area for young Christians to expend physical energy in a positive way and at the same time talk and reflect on the Lord. He convinced the church to invest $18,000 in weight-lifting equipment. This investment helped attract enough youths to build a mailing list of ten thousand. Rick learned firsthand how to attract bees by using a drop of honey.

As a part of his education, Rick was sent on a mission to Japan. It's been said that he memorized his Christian testimony in Japanese. Japanese is not an easy language to master, but true to form, Rick didn't let a tall task keep him from doing the Lord's work. This was what his father had taught him as a boy. Rick was merely doing in Japan what he had seen growing up in California: going out and evangelizing, regardless of how far the drive, or how bumpy the road.

During his time at California Baptist, Rick was influenced greatly by two people: Billie Hanks, Jr., and W. A. Criswell. Meeting these two individuals would play a large role in determining the direction Rick Warren took, and would lay the groundwork for what would one day become Saddleback Valley Community Church.

Billie Hanks, Jr., and W. A. Criswell

Billie Hanks, Jr., is the founder of the International Evangelism Association, based in Fort Worth, Texas. The association puts interns to work with those more experienced in Christian discipleship, to let them learn by observation. They practice "multiplication" discipleship theories by teaching Christians how to deepen their faith and then challenging them to pass that information onto others, so that they, in turn, take on the task of creating new disciples. The ministry is based on II Timothy 2:2: "And the things that thou hast heard of me among many witnesses, the same commit thou to faithful men, who shall be able to teach others also." Hanks's interns have gone on to become pastors, ministers, evangelists, Christian businessmen, professionals, and men and women in other fields who continue to spread the faith.

Hanks heard about Rick Warren through another disciple, Eddie Piland, who had met Rick at California Baptist. Eddie told Billie he should disciple Rick. Billie understood that, with all the people that Eddie had met, he wouldn't tell him about someone to disciple unless that person was a serious candidate. So Billie flew out to California to meet Rick.

Hanks met a young man who "looked and acted Californian"—tanned, with casual dress, a relaxed manner, and a California vocabulary. But he also saw fire in Rick's eyes when they talked about evangelism. He could see Rick wanted to do more for the Christian church. So Billie encouraged Rick to consider graduate studies at Southwestern Baptist Theological Seminary in Fort Worth, Texas.

Coincidentally, around that time, Rick had an experience that changed his life. He had been a great admirer of a pastor, also out of Texas, by the name of W. A. Criswell. Dr. Criswell headed the world's largest church at that time, the First Baptist Church of Dallas. In Rick's mind, Criswell was the greatest American pastor of the twentieth century, who had created the church model that was most imitated around the world. And in 1973, when Rick found out that Dr. Criswell would be speaking at the Jack Tar Hotel in San Francisco, he jumped at the chance to see him in person. It was a three-hundred-and-fifty-mile drive, and Rick would have to miss some classes, but he knew he had to take advantage of opportunity. He knew the Lord was bringing Dr. Criswell to the West Coast. It was up to Rick to accept His invitation to meet the legendary pastor. Rick and a friend embarked on the long drive up to San Francisco.

Dr. Criswell was the perfect public speaker. He had a

great manner, a singsong voice, and was a wonderful orator. He could pack houses, but more importantly, he could deliver a message that stuck. Rick sat and listened to Dr. Criswell in awe, and realized that he had made the right choice to come listen to him. Not only was he moved by the sermon, he was more convinced than ever that God was sending him a message: Rick Warren was to spend his life evangelizing.

After Dr. Criswell finished, he stood in line to shake everyone's hand, and Rick dutifully waited for his chance. As it turned out, his meeting with Criswell was more than he'd ever expected. The pastor didn't just shake Rick's hand—he looked at Rick and proclaimed, "I feel I need to lay hands on you and pray!" Criswell then said, "Father, I ask you give this young preacher double the portion of Your Spirit. May the church he pastors grow twice the size of the Dallas church. Bless him greatly, O Lord." The experience was a true epiphany for Rick. He knew then that he had to preach the Word. At that moment, the passion to build his own ministry seized Rick's soul.

Southwestern Baptist Seminary

Rick's evangelism in Japan, at the local church, and at school so impressed the faculty of California Baptist that they asked him to teach a class on evangelism his senior year. This gave Rick the opportunity to organize his evangelistic thoughts and theories. It also exposed students to an incredibly young minister-to-be, giving them a connection to the church of the future. Rick then took the next step in his ministry development process: he applied to and was accepted to Southwestern Baptist Theological Seminary in Fort Worth, Texas. He and Kay packed their belongings and headed east. They moved into a small frame house near the seminary, owned by Billie Hanks's association. Doing the Lord's work was literally taking Rick through Billie Hanks's backyard.

Founded in 1908, Southwestern Baptist was one of the most influential educational institutions in the Baptist Church: most of the significant pastors and important members of the church had attended seminary there. The school also had a major international reputation, training many of the missionaries serving in foreign countries. This combination of reputation and influence created an opportunity for people not only to strive for academic excellence, but also to become involved with the Baptist power structure.

When Rick arrived at Southwestern, the enrollment was up to five thousand, making it the largest theological school in the nation. Its considerable size fostered diverse opinions, even within the Christian community. During Rick's time at the seminary, there was a debate raging in the

Baptist church between "fundamentalists" and "modernists." The battle was between two opposing ideals: to honor the church by maintaining its traditions, or to change the church to suit the evolving world without sacrificing the fundamental message of the Lord. Rick stayed out of the fray, much as he stays out of such things today. (He does not contribute to, endorse, oppose, or take any positions on political issues inside or outside the church.)

Rick was careful to maintain a low profile at Southwestern. He was there to learn, not to show off. His entire focus was on quietly absorbing what was going on around him and applying it to his big-picture plan of building his own mega-church somewhere. Part of this planning process was finding out how other churches grew. Which concepts, when put into practice, made them larger? Rick wrote to one hundred of the biggest churches in the country and asked them what they did to be successful.

Gathering information from all the churches, he began to compare notes. What was the common pattern? What were the things successful churches did better than others? How did they reach the unchurched? What kind of a community were they successful in? What did they try that didn't work? Why didn't it? By asking all these questions and comparing the data to what he wanted to accomplish with his own church one day, Rick began to see a clearer picture.

Different Professors, Different Views of Rick

Rick's professors at Southwestern had different reads on Rick and his aspirations. Some professors could sense his ambitions, his fire, and his determination. Others didn't see that passion in his eyes—they just thought of him as a quiet, dedicated student. Both impressions are understandable. Rick is a low-profile person. It's only when you catch him in a moment of passion that his talents become obvious.

For example, Al Fasol, who taught a class called "Principles in Biblical Preaching," had Rick as a student for sixteen weeks. Al cannot recall if Rick contributed anything verbally to the class during that time. If he did, the comment, like Rick, did not stand out. The same goes for former Seminary President Russell Dilday, who noted that Rick was "more of a well-rounded 'B' type of student . . . not a standout type of person."

One of the factors that allowed professors to misjudge Rick was the fact that some of his classes didn't quite seem relevant to him at the time. Rick's Greek professor, Bruce Corely, said, "He would ask me why he had to take these Greek classes. It didn't make sense to him." Bruce Corely has subsequently visited Rick at the Saddleback Church, and is happy to know that his once skeptical student now understands why it was important to learn Greek twenty-five years ago. "The last time I saw him, he told me he wished he could take those classes again," Corely said. "What happens when you preach and teach over a long period of time is that you realize that knowing the Scriptures in the original language allows you to dig into the depths of their meaning." Bruce Corely has seen his once-questioning student now come full circle on the purpose of understanding Greek. Corely was also gratified to see how such an "ordinary" pupil could do so much work for God. And do it without changing his reserved, humble personality.

Professor C. W. Brister taught a class on pastoral leadership and pastoral administration. He recalls Rick being a very respectful student, always addressing him as "Dr. Brister." To Dr. Brister, Rick did not stand out in terms of academics. But there was something about Rick that separated him from the rest of the students: he thought like an entrepreneur. Rick was constantly promoting the idea that if you reach people and truly disciple them, they will do work for God.

Cal Guy, a former evangelism professor at the seminary, remembers Rick as a physically nondescript person. In reality, that's just the way Rick would like it: he wants his work to do the talking, not his appearance or stage presence. But one thing Guy couldn't help but notice about Rick was his absolute fire about evangelism. Rick might not have understood why he was taking Greek, but he certainly understood why he was taking evangelism. He soaked up everything his mind could absorb on the subject, in class and out.

In Rick's final year at the seminary, there were a couple of classes that really sparked his passion for learning. Guy created a new class on planting new churches. Rick signed up and, according to Guy, seemed to know more about the subject than he did. Another class that grabbed Rick's attention was "Teaching and Training Systems." Budd Smith taught that class, which was about using multimedia such as video and audio in making presentations. Smith claims that "Rick did such a fine job on his assignment that I used it as a model for subsequent classes and a mark against which they were measured. It was well packaged and very professional." Certainly neither Guy nor Smith ever had reason to doubt Rick's drive to succeed as a minister.

West Texas Ranch for Christ

In addition to working on his master's in divinity at Southwestern, Rick worked at the West Texas Ranch for Christ, Billie Hanks, Jr.'s training facility near Sweetwater. Rick and other young seminarians taught visiting college students, including those from Baptist student unions across the nation. "Rick was very active at the ranch. We would bring in young university students and go out and do house-to-house evangelism in places like Midland, San Angelo, and Sweetwater," recalls Hanks.

Rick was well loved at the ranch. Said Hanks, "Rick had a way of coming up with rhymes. He nicknamed my daughters Heather the Feather and Heidi the Mighty. Then he'd say, 'Heidi the Mighty, Heather the Feather, two sisters always together.'" He and Rick would play their guitars, laughing and singing and just enjoying the work they were doing. It became clear to Hanks that Eddie Pilland's comment years before about this young man was true to its mark.

It was also during his time at the ranch that Rick began writing books. He wrote two, both collaborative efforts. One was titled *The Victory Scripture Memory Series*, which he wrote with Billie Hanks, Jr., and Wayne Watts. The second was titled *Twelve Dynamic Bible Study Methods for Laity*, also written with Hanks and Watts.

Rick further took advantage of the dynamic learning situation he was in by refining some of the concepts he would make popular later. One time, everyone at the ranch was asked to share his or her favorite Scripture verse. Rick quoted Proverbs 14:4: 'Where no oxen are, the crib is clean; but much increase is by the strength of the ox." Billie Hanks said this illustrated what Rick called the, "NM principle in churches: No Mess, No Ministry." This relates directly to

Rick's belief that if a church is going to recruit new people, it's going to encounter problems related to those people being there. But it's the mission of the Lord to overcome such difficulties and create new disciples.

This is an important point, and is something Rick understood even as an aspiring pastor. He realized that the choice was not between being "traditional" and being "modern." The choice was rather between staggering to a slow death and dealing constructively with growing pains. Either path would be painful, but which one fulfilled the goal of evangelism? Which brought more people to Jesus? Rick believed it was the latter. Change is messy and painful at times. But without change, growth can't happen. Without growth, there are no new members. If you have no new members, you aren't evangelizing. If you aren't evangelizing, you are not doing the Lord's work.

One day during a class at the Texas Ranch, Billie asked Rick to teach. (Billie did this with all the interns in order to give them leadership training.) Rick walked up to the blackboard and drew a baseball diamond. Then he outlined what the diamond meant in terms of evangelism and church growth. Each base represented a step to the ultimate goal—evangelism, represented by home plate. This baseball metaphor would later become an important part of Rick's Purpose-Driven Church concept. We'll talk about this concept in detail in chapter seven.

A Rising Star

Billie Hanks was not surprised by Rick Warren's emergence as an evangelist. "Rick was so confident. He was so focused. He never doubted his calling. He wanted to go on changing the way the church went about its work, to make it more relevant to people. Those of us who believed in him and wanted him to succeed from the first day knew he would succeed. We all expected great things from him, and he has delivered well on those expectations." Nor was his success a shock to another one of his teachers, Roy Fish. Fish agrees with the observation that Rick never called attention to himself. "He would almost do anything he could to keep from standing out in a crowd. But when you got to know him, you would understand that this was the number one man. He always had such self-confidence and a tremendous self-image that he never felt it necessary to do that [grab attention]."

Fish says that Rick was an excellent pastor, even as a young seminarian. "I was interim pastor at Casa View Baptist Church in Dallas, and I thought enough of Rick to ask him to fill the pulpit for me when I was away. I still have the sermons he preached on tape. They were wonderful."

Rick also helped Fish put together a new class on discipleship evangelism. "Rick designed the curriculum for that course and I admitted it to the class. I got a lot more material from Rick than from any other source, even though he was a student in the class. It was about the principles of multiplication, disciple making, and reproducing disciples. He believed in doing exactly that and he is still doing it today at Saddleback. There are hardly any inactive members at Saddleback Community Church."

Fish adds, "Rick was the brightest student I knew by far, especially from the standpoint of church growth. I realized he knew more about that than most of his professors."

From the beginning, Roy Fish understood who Rick Warren was and what he could do, just as Rick understood what Roy was doing in his class. That mutual understanding was the basis of the profound respect the two men had for each other. Later, when Rick left for California, he told Fish that his goal was to go to Orange County and start a church that would grow to twenty thousand members. Fish said his former student still sends him autographed copies of his new books, calling the seminary professor his mentor. But Fish doesn't agree: "He was more of a mentor to me." And while he agrees that Warren's church growth principles are valid, Fish says the success of the Saddleback Church is not due to the methods, but to the man leading it. "The key to the whole thing is Rick. People can use his methods, but they won't get the same results."

Challenges

Not everything that happened to Rick while he was attending Southwestern was positive—there were some significant challenges, too. Some of the most severe problems had to do with his marriage. He and Kay were going through trying times. It got to the point where they agreed to go to professional counseling. They were so short on money (money being another one of the severe problems) that they had to charge the sessions on their Master Card. Today, Rick jokes about doing an ad for Master Card talking about how it helped save their marriage. As it turned out, their struggles and the perseverance to continue going forward doing the Lord's work, helped make their marriage stronger than ever.

Counseling and prayer weren't the only things that helped put Kay and Rick's marriage back on track. In his last year at Southwestern Baptist, Rick decided to take a trip to Southern California to visit Robert Schuller's Institute for Church Growth. Kay was skeptical—she didn't like the big-production approach to church. However, after meeting Schuller and understanding more about his ministry, Kay started to believe in his message. She never again doubted Rick's ambitions of starting a growth church.

The McGavran Influence

As noted before, while attending Southwestern Baptist, Rick did significant research into what it took to grow a church. His investigation pointed him in the direction of Donald McGavran, who was teaching at the Fuller Institute in Pasadena, California. McGavran, the son two missionaries, was born in India in 1897. He attended college in the United States before returning to India in 1923 as a missionary with the United Missionary Society.

In India, McGavran became curious about why churches grew so slowly, and he began studying that question. For the next seventeen years, he examined some 145 mission stations, and published his conclusion in a book, *The Bridges of God*, which was published in 1955. It was quite controversial at the time, and for some, it still is.

McGavran wrote that it is not enough for evangelists to sit around mouthing the Gospel and waiting for God to do something. Instead, he put the responsibility on Christians to do things that created disciples of God. The book called for Christians to be proactive rather than passive in their faith. McGavran also believed that the main task of the church was to bring nonbelievers into a committed relationship with Jesus Christ and into active fellowship in the church. Therefore, he advocated that the church embrace above everything else those things that actually produced disciples.

What McGavran was doing was calling for a return to the classical mission role of churches, stressing evangelism and church-planting ideas. These ideas dated back to the times when early Christians were establishing missions in primitive countries around the world. McGavran thought the same thing should be true in the present: whenever Christians went to a new part of the world, they should start a church, even if they had only the simplest of means. Starting a church shouldn't require special training or ordination. As McGavran put it, "You didn't have to have degrees from Harvard. If you loved the Bible and the Lord, you had the church."

McGavran thought the Christian Church needed to go back to that model. "We need to have people who really love the Lord. Now, I'm not against education. I myself am a graduate of Yale Divinity School and the Union Theological Seminary of New York. I have taught in nine seminaries . . . However, we need to have congregations that fit all kinds of people."

In 1960, McGavran was invited to establish an Institute for Church Growth on the campus of Northwest Christian College in Eugene, Oregon. Then in 1965 he received an invitation to come to Fuller Theological Seminary in

Pasadena, California, where he became the founding dean of the Fuller School of World Mission. In 1970, he wrote *Understanding Church Growth*, which takes the reader significantly further than *Bridges of God* in terms of McGavran's theories of evangelism, and reveals how his theories of church growth evolved. In a later book, *Effective Evangelism, A Theological Mandate*, McGavran proposed that Bible schools need to have required courses on evangelism. The basic ideas were the importance of leading "the lost" to existing churches and starting new churches. In McGavran's mind, all Christians should be New Testament Christians who believe God wants His lost children found.

McGavran's passion for church growth seemed to stem from his realization that an overwhelming majority of people—around three-quarters of the population, or possibly as much as four-fifths—are non-Christian. Many of those non-Christians are in North America. "A very large number of people have no connection with any branch of the Christian Church in spite of the fact that many in America think, 'Oh, everybody is Christian and belongs to some kind of church,' " said McGavran, "In fact, great numbers of people have no connection or only a slight connection with a particular church. For those of us in the Christian movement, therefore, there is an urgent need for new churches to reach into the population which is not being churched." That message—the need to reach the unchurched—would become the primary fuel behind Rick Warren's ministry.

Finding the Right Place

Rick Warren gained a lot from his experience at Southwestern. He acquired a top-notch education, honed his skills, and networked with people who had a real impact on his life and his ministry. Although he had to take some classes as requisites (Greek, for example), he was able to select classes and design a curriculum that pointed toward evangelism and church-building. He coauthored two books, helped with class material (evangelism), and even started to test-market his new concepts (the baseball diamond) at Hanks's West Texas Ranch. But just as important was the fact that during his time at Southwestern, Rick learned he didn't fit into the traditional church organization. Ebby Smith, a professor who had Rick in his ethics class, comments, "He would speak up in class, but he was much more interested in looking for where God wanted him to go. We talked about it a time or two. He was not like some of our students who wanted to go where there were well-established churches." Rick Warren wanted to do something new.

With the words of Criswell, the writing of McGavran,

and the encouragement of Billie Hanks, Jr., his course work at Southwestern, and of course the influence of his father, Jimmy Warren, Rick Warren knew he had found his purpose in life. "I felt God directing me to invest the rest of my life discovering and applying the principles that produce healthy, growing churches."

He had done his research, and plenty of critical thinking. A clear picture had emerged in his mind, and it looked like this:

- Evangelize: seek the unchurched and bring them to discipleship.
- Build a growth church and stay with it: churches that change pastors don't grow.

But some questions still remained. The biggest one was, Where would he take his ministry? If he was really going to seek the unchurched and create a growth church, he realized he had to find an area of the country with a growing population of unchurched people. Rick found that the areas of predominant growth at that time, the late seventies, were in Seattle, San Francisco, Orange County, and San Diego.

He investigated to see what was happening in the Baptist Church. He found that while the church was growing in rest of the nation, it was stagnant on the West Coast. The Southern Baptist fundamentalist view of the Bible did not seem to be well received there. But Rick saw one glimmer of hope, one area where his approach to Bible preaching might work: Orange County, California. That's where Rick decided to locate his new church.

Before he set his plan into motion, though, Rick had to get permission from the Southern Baptist Church. He wrote to Herman Wooten, the Southern Baptist director of missions, asking if he could start a Baptist church in Southern California. Coincidentally, at the same time, Wooten wrote a letter to Rick asking him if he would be interested in starting a church in Orange County. The two letters crossed in the mail. Rick had his answer before the question was asked.

In December of 1979, Rick and Kay Warren packed their belongings into a U-Haul and headed west with their baby daughter. Rick knew what he wanted to do. He knew where to do it. And he trusted that the Lord was guiding him to do the right thing. He soon found out just how right he was.

CHAPTER FOUR

DOING THE LORD'S WORK

RICK Warren is, without a doubt, one of the most successful pastors of what is known officially as the Church Growth Movement. He didn't get there overnight. Putting together a solid strategy to reach such a goal—building a mega-church with over sixteen thousand parishioners—didn't happen from taking one class at school. It didn't happen after a semester, either. It happened by feeding off positive passion to achieve his goal. For Rick Warren, the dream was to reach out and evangelize to as many people as possible. He had to do his homework, build relationships, and continually find creative ways to improve. As we shall see, this entrepreneurial spirit in church building is what makes Rick Warren's Saddleback ministry a success.

Starting the Congregation from Scratch

Arriving in Orange County, Rick Warren and family pulled their U-Haul into the first real estate office they saw. There they met an agent, Don Dale. Rick explained that he had just moved from Texas with his wife and infant daughter, he was in Orange County to start a new Baptist church, they needed a place to rent, and—by the way—they had no money. Dale not only found an apartment within the hour, but one that would rent the first month to the Warrens for free. Dale was so impressed with Rick that he also became the first member of Rick's congregation.

Now Rick had to take his first steps: garner resources and build the congregation. He solicited and received financial assistance from five Baptist churches and used his connections with Southwestern Seminary to bring fifteen students in to volunteer.

Rick was also careful to not step on any of the existing Baptist churches' toes. His philosophy was always to find the lost sheep—the unchurched. He reasoned there was no need to take other parishioners anyway because he knew the number of the unchurched far exceeded the supply of churches in the area.

Even with Orange County being a target-rich market

for Rick's church concept, it would take substantial effort and perseverance to build the congregation. Not being someone to waste a lot of time, Rick found a way to accomplish both tasks—finding them and convincing them to come in—with his first evangelism campaign. Rick and the volunteers went door-to-door in and around the Lake Forest community. The door-to-door approach served several purposes. First and foremost, it was a market survey to find out what kept people from going to church. If Rick could form a church that removed those excuses, then he could increase the likelihood that those people would attend church.

Through this door-to-door effort, Rick recruited enough people to form a Bible study group that met at his apartment. They also helped with the next step of the campaign—a mass mailing to fifteen thousand households. Again, Rick was targeting the unchurched and the reasons that kept people from going to church. His first letter opened with, "At last! A new church for those who have given up on traditional services!" Talk about attention-grabbing!

Next was to deliver on what was promised in the mailing: something different. But what? Rick realized that in order to bring in the unchurched, he had to speak to what was important to them, not preach at them on how they should live. To do this, he knew his sermons had to be written toward people who had turned away from going to church because of boring sermons. He wanted his sermons to invite them to experience God's love and gifts, and then to live a fulfilled life doing God's work—and doing it in an energetic, lively way. He wound up throwing out all but two of his sermons, and then he began to write new ones.

The goal of the congregation was to have their first service at Easter and to have 150 people attend. They needed a facility to host the service for that many people and were able to use Laguna Hills High School. They sent out fifteen thousand mailers announcing the first service at the high school on April, 6, 1980—Easter Sunday.

That morning, 205 people arrived for service at Laguna Hills. Robert Schuller had a total of 35 people at his first service in Dolton, Illinois. Watching these 205 new members stream in, Rick marveled, "This is really going to work!"

Even at his first sermon, he didn't just sit back and say thanks. Rick Warren announced his bold plans to build a church with twenty thousand members located on fifty acres of land. He was laying down the challenge to both himself and his congregation immediately. This was not going to be a passive church, and he was not going to be a passive pastor. They were going to grow, grow for the right reasons, and grow big. By letting people know from the very start what his aspirations were and where he wanted to go, he eliminated any second-guessing.

Rick made sure that his lofty goals did not send out the wrong signals to the unchurched community he was trying to reach. Material status—especially in terms of church appearance—was not important to Rick. Creating a church that had genuine warmth rather than museum coldness was what he wanted. He knew the unchurched were turned off by the material gaudiness of many churches. All of his services and meetings were in buildings that resembled anything but a church.

A true entrepreneur in church growth, Rick did not even use an actual church building until the church had ten thousand members. That milestone took fifteen years to reach. In the meantime, they had to scramble around the Orange County area to rent a total of seventy-nine different locations for church services and meetings. Even when they finally bought their own property to build on, they didn't erect a permanent building. They put up a tent, with no heating or air-conditioning (and it can get pretty hot in August in the Saddleback area).

Not only did Rick make people feel more relaxed by his casual building appearance, he helped people relax by dressing casually. Another barrier keeping people out of church was knocked down. Rick wears Hawaiian shirts when delivering a sermon—the same casual wear many people in the Southern California area have.

In addition to the content of sermons being written for

the unchurched, their duration was geared toward that group, as well. Rick broke up his sermons into fifteen-minute segments, interspersing them with music. And the music wasn't organ music that made the ears ring and the mind numb. It was modern instrumental music, mostly with guitars—music that moved and made the people feel a part of the celebration.

The time was right for Saddleback. The Orange County area population exploded in the 1980s and 1990s. Entire communities of twenty five thousand, such as Rancho Santa Margarita, sprang up and were filled with families—families in a new community that had no sense of community history, no community roots. The landing place for these people? Saddleback Valley Community Church, where they could join and participate in one of the over one hundred active service organizations in the church. They immediately could belong to a community group of their choice.

Pastor Rick Warren—Down-to-Earth Leader

Rick Warren is not a handshake type of guy. He's a warm, welcome-you-home hugger. He wears sockless sneakers to church along with his trademark Hawaiian shirt. His re-laxed, informal demeanor is not an act put on for Southern

Californians. It's the way he has always been—from the days of long hair and guitar playing at Ukiah High School, to his quiet, laid-back, reflective style at Southwestern. His manner has always been relaxed.

He's not an in-your-face, pound-the-pulpit preacher that threatens the congregation with lightning words punctuated by thunderous fists. The sermons delivered at Saddleback are for the people, not the preacher. Since they're for the people, they're real. Rick so effectively talks about his human side, his passion for Krispy Kremes, the mistakes he's made, and the challenges he's had in his marriage—that people naturally feel at ease with him.

People can trust him, so they trust what he says. That leads people to believe in the Word he is talking about—the Message of Jesus Christ. When people like what they see and hear, they tell others because they are excited about this different church. What does all of this do? It brings in more people, and the church grows. It doesn't grow because it's pushing into the community, but because it is inviting the community in to share and bond in the Word of the Lord.

Rick Warren created the Saddleback Valley Community Church following in the footsteps of his father's mission to reach out to people and invite them in to become a part of a community and help build a church. That has meant setting an example and avoiding the hazards that have victimized too many pastors. He refuses to accept money beyond his family's needs. He drives an old truck. The proceeds from his successful books have been used to pay back his entire salary over the last twenty-five years. A good portion of the rest of the book royalties go to charity.

His demeanor as the founder and pastor of one of the largest churches in the world reflects a man whose focus is on his mission to serve the Lord by bringing in the unchurched souls—the lost sheep—to embrace and celebrate the saving Grace of Jesus Christ. He doesn't crave the limelight, and actively avoids calling attention to himself. Holding no press conferences on the Supreme Court steps, he shuns any media coverage—whether it be radio or television. By doing this Rick Warren stays true to his congregation, true to his mission to do the Lord's work, and has earned the respect of many pastors and religious leaders.

An example of his down-to-earth approach to his ministry and life was recalled by Joe Fry, the pastor at Trinity Baptist in Ukiah. One time in the late eighties—after Rick had already gained significant notoriety with his Saddleback Church success—he was visiting Ukiah, and he and his gang decided to go frog-gigging with Joe and three other friends. They tried to figure out how to hunt the amphibians. The best way that came to mind was to have one person get behind the frogs in the pond and to try to "drive" them toward the people onshore. Well, guess who waded in the mud to be the "driver"? Rick Warren, the guy who always sets the example by rolling up his sleeves and getting involved. He wouldn't give someone a task he wouldn't do himself—another sign of a great leader.

That's what a lot of people don't understand about leadership. They think it's all about power or money or both. The ability to tell someone to do something and have them obey out of fear. Limo service to and from work, offices that resemble art galleries, and selling sizzle rather than substance. That's not leadership. That's not Rick Warren. He leads purely on the passion of his mission— to save one more for Jesus Christ.

The Church Growth Movement: Books and Bill Hybels

Not only did Rick figure out he had to change the message in his sermons, but he also knew he had to send his message through books. But there were other reasons to write books, too. First, he'd realized in his Southwestern days that another way to make sure he really knew where he was going was to write books about the tactics and strategies it took to get to the goal. By putting it into book form, he had to organize his thoughts so he could communicate them effectively.

GEORGE MAIR

Another good thing about books was that they spread the philosophies Rick Warren was developing on the Church Growth Movement. Rick's goal was to evangelize to as many as he could, but he realized he had to stay at his church if it was to grow. By writing books, he could aid other churches' growth without taking time from his own.

His most popular book by far is *The Purpose Driven Life*, which includes a step-by-step forty-day approach to a better life. It has sold over 20 million copies. (We'll discuss the book more in Chapter Seven.) Rich Karlgaard, publisher of *Forbes* magazine, called this book "the best book in entrepreneurship, business, and investment in a long time." He praised the business value and philosophy of Rick's work by comparing it to the growth of Dell or Starbucks. Karlgaard said the key to Rick's incredible success in selling books and growing Saddleback was his ability to "identify a consumer need—a religious consumer need—and fill it." That need was the need of the unchurched.

The best form of acceptance for the Church Growth Movement is replication. This holds especially true if it is done as an independent effort utilizing different resources in an entirely different market. Bill Hybels of Willow Creek Church near Chicago, Illinois, is one example of this.

Like Warren, Hybels is focused on unchurched people looking for answers to their problems in a church where they feel comfortable. To reach this seeker segment, Hybels followed the example of Gilbert Bilezikian, another pioneer in the church growth movement. An important part of Bilezikian's philosophy was the idea that the church should be a community of believers. (We'll talk more about Gilbert Bilezikian in Chapter Five.) Excited by Bilezikian's concepts of church in the community, Hybels recruited three friends and went surveying door-to-door in the Chicago suburbs, talking to people about whether they went to church, and why or why not.

Some of the answers from these hundreds of residents were predictable and some were not. Some said that church was boring, made them feel guilty, or that they didn't like being badgered for money. Others said, "get rid of the organ," "pad the seats," and "ditch the cross and other symbols that make people nervous." Though the suggestions might have seemed trivial, Hybels was smart enough to know that, trivial or not, they were issues people cared about. Instead of ignoring what the people said, Hybels took these suggestions and built Willow Creek Church, a church that some observers would label "God's answer to Wal-Mart."

In fact, Willow Creek Church has been lauded by Harvard Business School. In a distinctly flattering case study, the school sought to explain why this particular interdenominational evangelical church was booming. In less than fifteen years, Willow Creek grew from "a hole in an Illinois wheat field into the largest church in America." Each week, more than twenty thousand people attend its services, and each year they give nearly $15 million to the church to cover the salaries of the 192 full-time employees. Today, nearly fourteen hundred other churches in North America have joined the Willow Creek Association to learn how to adapt the "Willow Creek principles" to their own churches.

Entrepreneurship: The Business Fundamentals of the Church Growth Movement at Saddleback

If one were to look at a successful business enterprise—say Southwest Airlines—would it be so different from Saddleback? Herb Kelleher, founder and former chairman of Southwest, recognized a need, just as Rick Warren did. Kelleher realized that more people would be willing to travel by air if they could afford it, but he wouldn't sacrifice customer service. He wanted them to enjoy the experience and come back again.

What Southwest did was to revolutionize the airline industry for the traveler. Air travel has increased twentyfold since the early 1980s. People and families who couldn't afford to travel by air or take the time to drive could now fly Southwest. Southwest also succeeded by being intelligently frugal—eliminating meals and First Class, and using only one kind of aircraft, the Boeing 737. And they did all of this without sacrificing safety or customer service. They hired right and trained well, grooming people who helped make Southwest a great place to work and provided customers with great flying experiences and a friendly atmosphere. "You are now free to move about the country" was not just a slogan—it was a belief that transformed the travel industry.

Rick Warren is also an entrepreneur who has succeeded by being intelligently frugal. He doesn't spend borrowed money. Rather, he invests earned money, and he does it very carefully. He doesn't believe in building a big church and then finding the people to fill it up—he always finds the people first. Then, when he has reached a certain level, he builds the church. And when he does, his emphasis is on durability and functionality rather than something competing for a Frank Lloyd Wright Architectural Award.

This approach of "keeping things hungry" is an effective way to grow any enterprise several reasons. For one, when any organization gets big and has large sums of cash, it tends to get lazy. Everyone wants to solve problems by throwing money at them. That never works. Another problem with cash-fat organizations is that people working within the organization—in this case the church—lose sight of their purpose because they are so enamored with all the money. They lose the roll-up-the-sleeves-and-get-dirty ambition that made growth happen. Worst of all, they lose sight of their customers.

No matter how big Saddleback has gotten, Rich Warren has not lost sight of his "customer." Even though the church has grown to more than sixteen thousand members, new visitors still get the best parking spaces, are still personally greeted as they walk into the church. Rick wants them to feel welcomed, because bringing new people to Jesus is what it's all about to him.

Market Uniqueness

In his time at Saddleback, Rick Warren has also made sure to focus on a unique market, just as Southwest Airlines did. And like Southwest, he targeted a group of people who had never before experienced his particular product: a church that had no "First Class" seating, a church that made common people feel welcome, a church that gave them good service and fulfilled their spiritual needs.

By focusing on a unique market—the unchurched— Rick Warren was able to tap a vast resource without damaging relationships with other churches. As a result, other churches were willing to provide resources to Saddleback Church.

The fundamental concept behind what Rick Warren is

doing today is the same one that inspired his father, Jimmy Warren, Sr., in Northern California forty years before: evangelism. But one thing Rick Warren has learned is that, though the target market may be the same, what brings them to church is always changing.

CHAPTER FIVE

THE CHURCH GROWTH MOVEMENT

R ICK Warren and his Saddleback Church are important symbols of a larger-scale development in the Christian Church: the Church Growth Movement (CGM), also known as the Mega Church Pattern. A mega church is, by definition, a church with at least two thousand members (Saddleback has about sixteen thousand). The goal of churches that are part of the Church Growth Movement is to move away from the model of a small, traditional congregation of five hundred or so lifelong churchgoers. Instead, they operate on a more massive scale, striving to attract thousands of unchurched men and women and introduce them to Jesus.

In 1979, the year before Rick started the Saddleback

Valley Community Church, there were ten mega churches in the United States. The next year, the total leapt to fifty, and ten years later, in 1990, it had grown to three hundred churches. By 1999, there were five hundred mega churches in the country. Today, more than 1.7 million Protestants in America attend mega churches. Not surprisingly, many of those men and women are concentrated in Southern California, which, as noted before, had a particularly large population of unchurched people. To date, the ten largest mega churches in Southern California are:

1. Saddleback Valley Community Church—16,000 members

2. Los Angeles Church of Christ—13,400 members

3. Calvary Chapel Costa Mesa—12,000 members

4. Calvary Chapel Golden Springs—12,000 members

5. Harvest Community Fellowship—12,000 members

6. Grace Community Church—10,000 members

7. West Angeles Church of God in Christ—9,000 members

8. Crenshaw Christian Center—6,000 members

9. First AME Church—6,000 members

10. Mariners Church—6,000 members

The numbers speak for themselves. The Church Growth Movement has been wildly successful in Southern California (these ten churches alone total more than a million congregants), as well as in the rest of the country. Which prompts us to ask: what are the roots of this powerful movement? Rick Warren may be the foremost figure in the CGM today, but he's only a piece—albeit an important one—of a greater development in the Christian Church. Who and what gave birth to this movement in which Rick would play such a vital role?

Laying the Groundwork: New Age Preacher Norman Vincent Peale

Reverend Norman Vincent Peale is, to many, the most prophetic and moving New Age preacher of the twentieth century. He is also the father of the self-help movement that formed the groundwork for the Church Growth Movement. Peale formed perhaps the most dramatic and meaningful link between religion and psychology of any religious leader in history. It is this same approachable, therapeutic brand of religion that many mega churches, including Saddleback, put forward today. It is this kind of religion that is so appealing to the masses of unchurched men and women that Rick Warren hopes to reach.

Peale was born in 1898 to a Methodist minister and his wife in Bowersville, Ohio, into a family of modest means. He was originally ordained as a Methodist, but later became a Dutch Reform minister. In 1932 he had the opportunity to take over one of the most powerful and important parishes in New York City, the Marble Collegiate Church in Manhattan. There he would be a powerful influence on the Christian community for the next fifty-two years.

At Marble Collegiate, Peale accomplished two main feats. The first was, as noted before, melding psychology with religion. The second was expanding his influence far beyond the island of Manhattan by becoming a prolific book author. He penned forty one books, which were read around the world. His runaway best seller, *The Power of Positive Thinking*, published in 1952, remained on the best-seller list for almost four years. The book was reprinted in every major language in the world and ultimately sold around 20 million copies.

The Peale Ministry

Peale's ministry was characterized by positivity. He avoided negative thinking and never made threatening remarks, because he considered them counterproductive to the goals he sought to achieve as a Christian. He avoided talking about injustice in the world, something we associate with Christian leaders—he didn't want anything negative infringing on his upbeat views. He rarely talked about his association with conservative politicians because he felt politics were outside the realm of religion.

Peale's resolve to have a positive attitude stemmed from experiences in his own life. As a young man, he was filled with fear and self-doubt. But then, one day in college, he resolved to change the way he viewed the world and his own life. He said that he found the solutions to all of his insecurities in the biblical revelations of Peter.

Realizing that the way he was being taught was not how he wanted to minister to others, Peale proclaimed that he would take a new road in his life. Out of that change in mentality and attitude was born his concept of *The Power of Positive Thinking*. The concept was that, through prayer, one could create a positive mind-set that would result in a positive being. The rewards of that mind-set would be spiritual, emotional, and physical riches.

Peale was able to communicate this idea to people by telling stories that were accessible, interesting, illuminating, fulfilling, and about real men and women. Essentially, his sermons and writings were about actual people he knew who'd suffered from problems, and how they solved them. It was a marvelous communication technique that Rick Warren would later adopt in his own ministry.

Carol R. George wrote a biography on Peale in 1992 entitled *God's Salesman*. In it, she reduced Peale's technique to three basic parts: picturize, prayerize, and actualize. When faced with a problem, a person should create a picture of the desired outcome—becoming healthy, getting money, being promoted, having a sick relative recover—whatever it may be. Then he or she should pray to God for that desired result and to learn what God's will is in that situation. Finally, he or she should do what has to be done in the physical world to bring about God's will.

Peale's mixture of Christ and Freud—Christianity and psychiatry—made his philosophy a worldwide success in both his preaching and his forty one books. His positive and active form of belief involving prayer, self-analysis, and directed religious energy helped people to gain control of their own lives. His message was described in a *Christian Community* article by Richard Pierard as "A composite of

Science of Mind, metaphysics, medical and psychological practice, old-fashioned Methodist evangelism, and Dutch Reformed Calvinism."

Valerie Takahama, writing in the *Toronto Star*, said, "The impulse toward self-improvement and that practical, can-do spirit helped Norman Vincent Peale's *The Power of Positive Thinking* become one of the highest-selling spiritual books of all time—and one of the most successful books of non-fiction on any subject." Widely acknowledged as one of the first self-help books, *The Power* set the standard for the thousands of other volumes that have followed in its wake—from *I'm OK—You're OK*, the classic 1969 book about transactional analysis by Thomas A. Harris, to *The 7 Habits of Highly Effective People*, Stephen R. Covey's 1990 best seller.

The Peale Effect

It was hard to find anyone who didn't have an opinion about Peale during his years at Marble. The general public embraced his simple, straightforward ideas. "His genius was in the simplicity of his message," said American religious historian Randall Balmer. "That message fit the tenor of the times in the middle decades of this century. It was a message of hope, optimism, and American middle-class values."

Balmer said that Peale was "probably directly or indirectly responsible for everything from Robert Schuller to the prosperity gospel." Carol George suggests that many motivational speakers, including Dale Carnegie and Zig Ziglar, are indebted to Peale. She attributes his enormous influence to the fact that he focused on ordinary problems in the lives of ordinary people, instead of debating how many angels can dance on the head of a pin as ancient monks used to. She also commented that Peale understood what turned off ordinary people. "He knew that to talk about sin, suffering, and guilt was not going to produce the attendance numbers he wanted."

Of course, not everyone embraced Peale's message. Many established, traditional Christian priests and scholars saw his words as a threat to their way of life. Many religious thinkers considered his approach too simplified—they saw religion and communion with God as not only a ritualistic, but also a private affair. The reverent worshiper should pray solemnly in a quiet, reflective setting. If God became too easy to reach—the equivalent of a spiritual 9-1-1—then who would need a pastor or priest or rabbi or shaman?

Some of Peale's former colleagues and another minister went so far as to accuse him of plagiarism. Writing in the *Lutheran Quarterly*, Reverend John Gregory Tweed of Fort Lauderdale, Florida, and Reverend George D. Exoo of Pittsburgh wrote that many of Peale's uplifting affirmations originated with an "obscure teacher of occult science" named Florence Scovel Shinn. They based this charge on their comparison of words in Peale's writings and those of Shinn's book, *The Game of Life and How to Play It,* in which they found some identical phrases.

Peale's association with Shinn offended some conservative and fundamentalist Christians. The editor of *Lutheran Quarterly,* Dr. Oliver Olson (a religious professor at Marquette University), felt compelled to publish the Tweed-Exoo article because some of his students were Dutch Reform (as Peale was) and were upset with the pastor's affiliation with what they considered to be ungodly hocuspocus. These students objected to his new feel-good, do-good, make-good teachings, and wanted to discredit Peale's message as "religious rubbish" by connecting it with ancient occult mysticism. Olson said these students believed that "The real biblical message is that the normal condition for people is sin, rebellion, and guilt, and the overcoming of such things is to repent," and not merely the pagan "feel-good" message of Peale's.

According to George, though, Peale was fully aware of the fact that his colleagues in the field criticized him for not being as intellectual as a prominent minister should be—he just didn't care. He didn't want to be overly scholarly or profound. As George said, "He was interested in everyday issues facing ordinary people."

Peale's ministry was the first to raise the question that still faces mega churches today: is it spiritual compromise if a pastor simplifies his message in order to make it appealing to a huge number of seekers? Does having color TV monitors in church somehow diminish the importance of the Good News? Certain self-titled "purists" would say so. But Peale didn't; nor does Rick Warren today.

It's been over ten years since Norman Vincent Peale died on Christmas Eve of 1993, but his name and his mission still stir controversy. His biographer, George, says, "Norman Vincent Peale is undoubtedly one of the most controversial figures in modern American Christianity." But no matter what people think about his theories, they have to acknowledge Peale's remarkable unification of psychology and theology. Without that unification, mega churches wouldn't exist today. Rick Warren's Saddleback Valley Community Church is just one of many mega churches that offer focus groups for a variety of social problems, including such topics as marriage, work, child rearing, substance abuse and dependency, depression, and other issues once thought to be beyond the scope of the Sunday church service. In that sense, Saddleback distinctly bears the stamp of Reverend Norman Vincent Peale.

The Fathers of the Church Growth Movement: McGavran, Bilezikian, Schuller

There are many theories as to where the Church Growth Movement began, and even more about who started it. Some people pinpoint its birth in the New Testament's Acts of the Apostles. Others cite such luminaries such as John Wesley. There seems to be some consensus, though, about the three men who played the largest roles in cultivating the CGM: C. Donald McGavran (who we discussed in chapter three), Gilbert Bilezikian, and Robert Schuller.

As we know, McGavran challenged young church leaders with the idea that "Unless we grow, we are not really doing God's business. Unless we are bringing in the lost, we are not really doing God's business. Unless we can find those who are poor sinners and make them saints, we are not doing our work." Bilezikian challenged them with another fundamental growth concept: that the church should be a community of believers. "Without community, there is no Christianity," he said.

Bilezikian was born in Paris, France, just before World War II, and grew up under the Nazi regime. In 1961, he made his way to the United States, where he became a minister and a teacher at Wheaton College in Wheaton,

Illinois. At Wheaton, Bilezikian developed his concept of the mega church. His emphasis was on bringing worshipers together in small groups—he felt that participating in small groups allowed people to help each other along in their missions. A key aspect of Bilezikian's concept was that "Christianity is not about being served but about serving." He believed that every man and woman in a church congregation had a ministry of his or her own, and that everyone—even church leaders—had to be ready to serve others and to help others learn to serve. Rick Warren incorporates this fellowship approach to ministry at Saddleback today.

Robert Schuller is the third person that claims credit for creating the mega church concept. He wrote in *The Christian Century* (April 10, 2002), "I have been credited or blamed—both are correct—as the founder of the mega church." He envisioned a church of roughly six thousand members who would generate enough revenue to support a staff of ten to twelve people. Schuller maintained that his idea was revolutionary because, in those days, mainstream denominations only planned small churches of no more than four hundred members. They thought that was the biggest number one pastor could accommodate.

"I launched the mega church movement through the Institute for Successful Church Leadership in 1970," Schuller said, referring to his annual pastors' conference at the Garden Grove church. "There were no mega churches thirty two years ago—we were the closest thing to it."

Lyle Schaller, author of several books about the Church Growth Movement, maintains that Schuller was *not* responsible for creating the mega church concept. "Historically, that's simply not true," Schaller says. He claims that if the mega church started anywhere, it was in Akron, Ohion, where at least two of the largest Protestant churches in America were located in the 1960s: Akron Baptist Temple and Rex Humbard's Cathedral of Tomorrow. In addition, downtown Dallas's First Baptist, First Presbyterian, First Methodist, and First Christian were "among the largest churches in their denominations," typically drawing two thousand or more people at worship services. The First Baptist Church of Dallas was, of course, run by Rick Warren's mentor, the Reverend W. A. Criswell.

But perhaps Schaller and Schuller are both correct in their assertions. Schaller may be correct as to who was first *chronologically*. But it's hard to argue that Schuller was not the first person to be *effective* on a national scale. He was unquestionably a pioneer in the Church Growth Movement and a major influence on Rick Warren. For that reason, we need to take a closer look at his story.

Reverend Robert Schuller

Robert Schuller was once quoted as saying, "You can always get to somewhere when you start at nowhere." "Nowhere" was how he characterized the Iowa farm where he was born on September 16, 1926, and raised until he was a young man. He referred to it as "the dead-end of a dirt road that had no name and no number."

In the early 1950s, after he had been ordained a minister at Western Theological Seminary, Robert Schuller married Arvella DeHaan and moved to Chicago. His first parish was the Ivanhoe Reform Church of Dolton, Illinois, on the south side of Chicago. It had thirty five members.

From the start, Schuller had long-term goals. He wanted to slowly and steadily build his church over the next forty or fifty years. To increase membership, he did something most people would never expect of a minister: he went calling on people in his community door-to-door like a magazine salesman, encouraging them to come to church on Sunday. His initial campaign saw limited success—people would typically attend church the following week, but disappear afterward. At first, Schuller couldn't figure out why people weren't sticking around. His wife, Arvella, though, understood. Her husband ringing doorbells during the week was novel and intriguing; his sermons on Sunday weren't.

Arvella candidly told Robert that his sermons were boring. They were too serious, she said, and weren't connected to the audience. "Whom are you trying to impress?" she asked. But she already knew the answer: her husband was trying to impress his professors back at school who had taught Robert how to preach, but not how to communicate or make a connection to ordinary people.

To remedy the problem, Schuller turned to two of the most popular works of the era about communication. One was *How to Win Friends and Influence People* by Dale Carnegie; the other was Norman Vincent Peale's *The Power of Positive Thinking*. Although intellectuals looked down on the theories of "popular" communication that the works espoused, both books were widely read by the public. That only meant they were perfectly suited to Schuller's new plan.

Schuller's investigation into the two books led to a spiritual rejunvination—a complete transformation into a minister who could "preach positive." And the effect was astonishing: his rapport with his parishioners and his main target, unchurched men and women, grew dramatically. Robert finally came to understand that sermons were meant not to convert, but rather to encourage and uplift people.

In the next four years, Schuller's parish grew from

thirty five to more than four hundred. In 1955, he accepted an invitation from church elders to head a mission in an uncharted territory, Orange County, California (which, at the time, also boasted another new enterprise called Disneyland).

Schuller's first goal after arriving in Orange County was to locate a building in which to house his ministry, but the only reasonable place he could find was a drive-in movie theater. After negotiating with the owner, he struck a deal to rent the theater for $10 a Sunday. On March 27, 1955, Reverend Schuller held his first "drive-in" service standing on the roof of the snack bar before an improvised cross. Arvella played an organ mounted on a trailer; a choir from another church sang. The service drew about fifty cars and a little over $83 in contributions. The ministry was on its way.

Those were trying times for Schuller. Sometimes the tarpaper roof of the snack bar got so hot that melted tar would stick to his shoes. He was often showered by rain and blasted by hot Santa Ana winds sweeping across the area. It was all Arvella could do to keep the wind from blowing her sheet music away. But they persevered. Six months later, Schuller's drive-in congregation had reached 144 members, and California officially declared the existence of a new church. The reverend chose the name for his parish, the Garden Grove Community Church, very carefully. He wanted a pleasant-sounding name that wouldn't alienate prospective parishioners.

Soon, Garden Grove was able to buy two acres of ground nearby and begin planning to build their own chapel. But as the project moved forward, Schuller realized that he might lose many of his drive-in parishioners if he shifted completely to a regular chapel. He decided to have two church locations and to hold two services every Sunday: one at the new chapel and another at the original drive-in location two miles away. This allowed Garden Grove to expand into new areas while maintaining the comfort and needs of his original parishioners.

Even as his church began to see large-scale success, Schuller faithfully continued his door-to-door solicitations. He once estimated that he personally rang thirty-five hundred doorbells. He also said he had the door slammed in his face too many times to count, and was routinely insulted both personally and religiously, but he kept looking for unchurched men and women who might come to services on Sunday. In so doing, he learned valuable lessons about people's attitudes, what they looked for and expected from a church, and even a few lessons about what God expected of Schuller himself. He continually worked to apply these lessons to his ministry. Perhaps the most valuable thing he learned in the process was humility, a trait that Rick Warren values above almost everything else.

Just two years after his first Sunday service, Schuller took a chance and invited Norman Vincent Peale to fly out from New York and preach to his congregation. In a move that stunned Schuller and the entire Southern California religious community, Peale accepted. On the morning of June 30, 1957, one of the most renowned preachers in America stood alongside Robert Schuller on the tarpaper roof of the Orange Drive-in Theater and preached to an overflow crowd. People were doubling up in their cars with complete strangers to be part of a religious presentation the likes of which they'd never seen before.

The most important aspect of the sermon Peale delivered was its trademark positivity, which deeply impacted all his listeners that morning—even the Dutch Reformist boy from the dead-end, no name, no-number dirt road in Iowa who had himself grown to be an important religious leader. Peale said, "Any human being can be anything he wants to be through the power Jesus Christ brings into his life!" After that day, Schuller's preaching was never the same.

"I followed his teachings and his message of positive thinking, and I called it 'possibility thinking,' Schuller says. "I moved it ahead . . . and turned it into a television program called *Hour of Power*, which is the most widely viewed televised church service in the world today."

In 1969, Schuller decided to try a new way of "spreading the word": he developed a program to teach other pastors what he had learned in his years of founding and developing his ministry. The Robert Schuller Institute for Successful Church Leadership put a small ad in the *Los Angeles Times* announcing its first program series, the first of its kind in America. Seventy-eight area ministers enrolled.

The central lesson Schuller delivered to this first group of pastors refuted traditional Christian theory calling for small congregations and ministries dedicated to the needs of the church and the religiously committed. He told the preachers to become missionaries to the unchurched, and to drop denomination labels from their church names. Schuller urged them to focus on the concerns of their parishioners while leaving the church establishment to take care of itself. One of the early participants in the Schuller Institute was Bill Hybels of the Willow Creek Community Church in Illinois. Later, another participant would be Rick Warren of Saddleback Valley Community Church.

Robert Schuller's evangelism soon exploded onto the national scene. Between his famed *Hour of Power* program, the fabled Crystal Cathedral he built that was designed by world famous architect Richard Neutra, and his numerous best-selling books, including *Move Ahead with Possibility Thinking*, *Self-Love*, and *Living Positively One Day at a Time*. Schuller left an indelible impression on the Church Growth Movement.

Going Forward

In the 1970s, others active in the Church Growth Movement included Win Arm, who established the Institute of American Church Growth, and John Wimber, who became the founding director of the Department of Church Growth at Fuller (now known as the Charles E. Fuller Institute of Evangelism and Church Growth). In the 1980s, C. Peter Wagner emerged as a major spokesman for the CGM, publishing some forty books on the subject. Bill Hybels is another one of the movement's most important thinkers. But in the 1990s, following in the footsteps of Peale and Schuller, the leader of the next generation of Church Growth Movement pastors emerged. That man was none other than Rick Warren.

CHAPTER SIX

THE NEW PARADIGM CHURCH: MODERN RELIGION IN AMERICA

I T'S clear that religion in present-day America is in a state of transition. What isn't clear is where that transition is heading. Will religion "settle out" anywhere into some defined, sustained approach to worship? Will it continue to splinter and divide? Will an entirely new form of worship arise? The one thing that's certain is that, right now, religion in America is growing and merging with new sectors of society and culture on a large scale. The success of the Church Growth Movement is evidence of that fact, as are other indicators. For example, sales of religious books are higher than they've ever been. After being shunned by profit-minded movie studios that feared it wouldn't draw, Mel Gibson's *The Passion* had record-breaking box office receipts.

This trend certainly has to do with the fact that worldwide violence, particularly violence based on religion differences, is escalating. And for Americans, it has to do with September 11. In the aftermath of the tragedy, people have become more curious about other faiths. The need to understand the roots of the world's conflicts has led to an increased desire to learn about religion. But the larger effect of the 9/11 tragedy has been the new quest for comfort from the fear generated by the attacks. The sudden realization that the world changed forever on that tragic day gave many men and women cause to reconsider. Suddenly, life was bigger, more important, and in dire need of explanation. Many looked for those answers in church.

America is a unique world in the way that it fosters religious growth. Here religions can grow unhindered, be created unquestioned, and exist unchallenged. Few other countries provide this opportunity for diverse religious development. Our ingrained sense of free-market capitalism has contributed to spiritual growth, too. Churches here not only have to compete with other religions to attract new members, they have to compete against all the other ways people can choose to worship besides going to church.

As a result, religious growth in America is more heavily weighted to new churches and religions than to traditional religions. Randy A. Nelson is a director of contextual education at Lutheran Seminary in St. Paul, Minnesota. In the July-August 1998, issue, of *Sojourners Magazine*, he wrote:

> A key point about religion in America today is that the main religious denominations have had little growth and, in some cases, fewer members. At the same time, Americans' interest in religion has sharply increased. Rather than being contradictory, the presence of these two trends suggests that a reasonably important shift may be occurring in the expression Americans give to their religious beliefs. Mainline churches are only one of the options available and increasing numbers of persons are seeking alternative forms through which to express their spirituality.

One of those new churches is Rick Warren's Saddleback Valley Community Church.

New Paradigm Churches

Donald Miller, a professor of religion at the University of Southern California, uses the phrase "new paradigm church" to describe the entity American churches are evolving into. Successful new paradigm churches are the mega churches in Southern California built by Robert

Schuller, and of course, Rick Warren. Miller says the popularity of these churches stems from their very distance from the traditional parish style. Mainstream churches, often overloaded with bureaucratic structure, aren't able to offer immediate solutions to their parishioners' problems or offer them in-depth guidance. Their response to issues often seems to be "Read the Bible and figure it out for yourself." By contrast, new paradigm churches are able to address people's concerns and reduce their stress while giving them a feeling of religious fulfillment. As we know, Rick Warren's Saddleback Church offers a variety of life management services. Groups and counselors are available to attend to such issues as sexual relationships, child-raising, teen drug and alcohol abuse, healthy teen alternative lifestyles, caring for the sick and aged, and coming to terms with the inner self. New paradigm churches are interested in the fulfillment of the people who attend, not the church structure itself.

The new paradigm churches have become a spiritual shopping mall for people searching for life's answers. With abundant choices of "stores"—focus groups, help groups, and ministries—from which to select, they will more than likely find at least one option that suits their needs. This multiple-ministry approach employed by new paradigm churches gives the individual the opportunity to select a group or program based on a specific need.

Traditionalists disdain such practices, labeling them "cheap merchandizing." But Dr. Miller counters with the idea that "the real staying power of new paradigm churches is that they are mediating deeply felt religious experiences and doing this much more effectively than mainline churches." Miller goes on to say that these new paradigm churches are doing "significant cultural repair—affirming the importance of children, conveying the need for each person to be responsible for his actions, and committed to helping each other praise God." He concludes by stating that mainline churches must give the church back to the people so that people can improve their lives.

One of the manifestations of the trend toward new paradigm churches is a change in church nomenclature. New churches are careful to avoid names and terms that are affiliated with specific denominations—words like "Baptist," "Evangelical," and "Dutch Reform." These churches don't want the old "brand name" religious label to turning off potential worshipers. Norman Vincent Peale and the Reverend Robert S. Schuller are examples of famous pastors who aren't affiliated with a specific denomination. Instead they are known for who they are, what they did, and how well they did it. Essentially *they* became the religious brand, rather than their churches. As it turned out, this brand-neutering concept would be an important part of Saddleback's success.

When Rick Warren started his yet-unnamed church in 1980, he and his leaders conducted several focus groups. What they discovered was that the word "Baptist" did not go over well with many people, particularly with the unchurched population. "Every response was negative," says Saddleback's executive pastor, Glen Kreun. He continued to say, "You just have to use words people appreciate." They finally settled on Saddleback Valley Community Church.

What Warren realized was that eliminating religious nomenclature meant that people didn't get bogged down into thinking about specific nuances of a religious sect, whether is be Baptist, Methodist, Presbyterian, Lutheran, or Episcopalian. Those names make it easy for people to assume they wouldn't fit in, especially if they've done some research into what each denomination stands for. New paradigm churches eliminate that problem—in fact, they eliminate the need to do religious "homework" completely.

Another effect of the paradigm shift toward mega churches is the cultivation of a more relaxed religious atmosphere. Traditional church services are formal affairs with organ music and robed choristers; new churches are dress-casual with upbeat music played by contemporary musicians. The sermons are less academic and more motivational, and at times earn a thunderous response from the live congregation.

Having a "community" or "fellowship" church instead

of another old denominational title makes that church less threatening to seekers. Historian Randall Balmer of Barnard College says older churches too often seem antiquated and out of touch with the modern world. As an alternative, Rick Warren and his advocates offer a church that is first and foremost focused on the worshiper, instead of the church establishment. That is the true definition of a new paradigm church.

God on the Mall

A sign of the extent to which churches are seeking new ways to connect with people is the "church on the mall" concept. Writing in Good Housekeeping (December 1, 1997), Jan Jarboe Russell says what is happening is that ministers and churches are taking God to the people instead of the reverse. Mr. Russell reports, "Some churches have established places of worship in shopping malls as a way to reach busy people. The Copperfield Baptist Church holds services in a suburban movie theater outside Houston, Texas. The Reverend Larry Womack says he wants to create a spiritual presence amidst materialism."

For Reverend Womack, putting a church in a commercial location allows people to combine their day-to-day and religious lives, bringing their belief in God with them instead of separating the two as if they had no relevance to each other. Rick Warren and his colleagues have found that to be an effective way of targeting the unchurched. Reverends Schuller and Warren went door-to-door to find unchurched men and women in their own neighborhood; Reverend Womack is seeking them out where they shop at the mall. His eleven-thousand-square-foot operation is sandwiched between a sports bar and a used bookstore. His location puts his congregation in the middle of what must be a rather interesting window-shopping experience: watch the Astros, worship, and then browse the works of Dickens.

Another mall minister is the Reverend John Chell. His church is located in the largest mall in the country—the Mall of America in Bloomington, Minnesota. His view is that Americans are busy people and churches have to make it easy for them to worship. Chell reasons that the shopping mall is a normal part of American life today. Why keep God isolated from where the people naturally congregate? To make the concept appeal to a larger demographic, Chell helped organize the Mall Area Religious Council (MARC) along with a Catholic priest and Methodist pastor (Chell is Lutheran). Now MARC is composed of twenty-three different denominations and sponsors an interfaith shop, the Meaning Store. The store sells books, artifacts, and other religious gift and novelty items. Chell says, "By being on the mall, we expand the definition of the word 'church' to something that involves people every day, not just one day a week."

Russell's *Good Housekeeping* story notes, "For the most part, mall churches are Christian, but they differ from other Christian churches in that they consist of mainly Baby Boomers who are disenchanted with the established religious authority and practices." He further notes that most Baby Boomers are running incredibly tight daily schedules—shuttling from soccer practices to music lessons to schools to jobs to shopping trips. Mall churches allow "church visits" to fit conveniently into the daily planner between going to the "shoe sale" and "shopping for groceries."

Dr. C. Peter Wagner, Fuller Theological Seminary professor in Pasadena, California, considered one of the leading authorities on mega churches, attributes even greater importance to the mall church concept. He points out that although communities of the past worshiped at traditional white steeple churches, more often than not those churches were located in the town square—the original version of "the mall." In his mind, the idea of going to the town center to work, buy goods, socialize, govern, and pray has been around for hundreds of years. It was only when the town economies shifted away from the squares to outlying factories and when churches started to flee to the solitude of the countryside that the original concept of "convenience worship" deteriorated. So having a centralized church may not be such a novel concept after all. Only today, shopping malls have replaced town squares.

Change vs. Status Quo

The mall church concept has its critics. The Reverend William Willimon, dean of the chapel at Duke University in Durham, North Carolina, says the concept of church at the mall is "appalling. I understand the impulse to reach out to where the nonbelievers go, but the church is not a store and the values we are selling are absolutely the opposite of the values represented by the mall." Willimon insists that the teachings of Jesus, which are focused on social equality, are in direct conflict with the idea of a free market economy where the rich get richer and the poor get poorer. His statement is, in many ways, a summary of the entire "fundamentalist" versus "modernist" division in the Christian church—less about philosophical differences on how and where to worship and more about clinging to the status quo or embracing change and evolution.

But if we assume that everything, including religion, needs to be able to change in order to survive, then it becomes clear that status-quo churches are only destroying what they are so desperately trying to hold on to. Though the success of the mall church model can't be completely equated to Rick Warren's success at Saddleback, they share the passion for growth and change that some older churches lack. They are willing to take risks, to challenge the "if it ain't broke, don't fix it" crowd. They look to capitalize on untapped resources: the population of the unchurched. Most importantly, they've taken into account what that population wants. These are men and women who have moved from where they grew up. They've changed jobs. They have spouses from different cultural or religious backgrounds. They see the white steeple not as a beacon of hope, but as a sign that says, "You don't belong in our group." Even though that's certainly not the intent of a traditional church's pastor or congregation, the success of the Rick Warren ministry makes it clear that significant numbers of people are turned off by traditional church settings and structures.

Television and Religion

We've discussed movies, the Internet, and multimedia presentations as ways to disseminate the Word of Jesus, but what about television? Certainly television has played a role in promoting (and sometimes ridiculing) Christian evangelism. Pat Roberts, Benny Hinn, and Jerry Falwell have used television as a major distribution and marketing media for their ministries. Despite their success, for many years networks fought to keep religious shows off of prime-time programming. "Religion is the last frontier that commercial television was willing to foray into," said Robert Thompson, professor of media and popular culture at Syracuse University. "[It] was the one place they steered clear of. Popular culture was supposed to comfort people. Religion, the idea went, made people uncomfortable."

Today, however, those walls are beginning to break down. Teresa Blythe, co-author of *Watching What We Watch: Prime-time Television Through the Lens of Faith*, says TV writers are creating story lines that involve a variety of religions. Two notable examples are *The West Wing* portraying a praying president and *Judging Amy* featuring a devout bailiff. Ms. Blythe ventures the opinion that in their depiction of religion TV writers will soon be bolder on the air than many pastors are from the pulpit. Does this necessarily signal a greater religious awareness on commercial television? Probably not. The reality of commercial TV is that it exists to make money. If a few religious themes and story lines help the networks achieve that goal, they'll use them.

Regardless of motivation, though, the religious trend in television is certainly a boon to the Christian Church. The faith message is being subtly and appealingly delivered. Religion in prime-time programs may well encourage people to attend church, which would be an unexpected bonus for Rick Warren's ministry.

Saddleback: A Truly Modern Church

One of the most important aspects of the new paradigm church movement is the reduction of church bureaucracies. Church organizations and their administrative structure had started to resemble government agencies, where each department created its own little fiefdom. They held meeting after meeting; their thinking became stagnant and inbred; worst of all, they lost track of why people were going to their church.

Newer churches, and mega churches like Saddleback in particular, have fewer administrative layers, less structure, and distribute more decision accountability to every level. This allows them to move on initiatives more quickly and to rapidly adapt to change—they don't get stuck in their own quicksand like large bureaucracies. Rick Warren's church finds burcaucracy to be stifling. And even though Warren uses corporate terms like "fill on demand," "downsizing," "merchandizing," "team players," and "niche marketing"—he's really striking at the heart of what makes certain corporations fail and others succeed: efficient customer service. The University of Southern California's Dr. Miller says, "Saddleback attends to consumer demand by fine-tuning their worship and organizational style to today's culture, not the cultures of the past."

A key difference between older churches and new paradigm churches like Saddleback is that the older churches tend to "focus on Sunday" operations, whereas the newer churches spread Sunday out over the entire week. They hold meetings, seminars, bring in guest speakers, do charity work, and run community outreach programs throughout the week.

Like any good corporation, Warren's ministry does not cater to everyone. His is an interactive church concept of mutual, unconditional giving. Anyone who wishes to exploit or challenge this philosophical approach is asked to leave Saddleback. It's a challenge for any large organization: the sheer numbers increase the odds that someone can "slip" in and cause significant problems. But it makes no sense for the church to welcome people who, by their actions, undermine its ability to evangelize. This strict policy keeps the massive congregation on target.

The Future of the Church Growth Movement

What does the future hold for Rick Warren and his flock? The world is rapidly changing: globalization, technology, an aging population, and a new generation are putting down roots. To keep pace with the changes, Rick plans to take Saddleback global. His focus initially will be on expanding churches in Latin America and Asia. As he first did in Southern California, he is looking to where the market of opportunity has a large potential growth and a high degree of acceptance.

Part of this global push will be made over the Internet. Saddleback's effort on this front is twofold. One aspect is to help pastors anywhere in the world to build a better church in terms of design, concept, and message for their worshipers. The other is to provide a resource of spiritual guidance for those who do not have or physically cannot attend a local church. These are the people Rick's dad, Jimmy Warren, Sr., always took time to find. Saddleback will accomplish the same thing, and in even more remote locations, riding the fiber-optic highway of the Internet.

The first group of baby boomers—the original group Rick Warren targeted when he founded Saddleback—is now approaching retirement age. Both Saddleback and the Church Growth Movement as a whole will have to create programs that adapt and cater to this change. The values of rebellious sixties youth generation have changed; to assume these people still want today what they wanted in the 1980s would a big mistake for a mega church. Saddleback is working with focus groups to determine what is important to these people *now*, not what was important ten, twenty, or forty years ago.

As the boomers age, a new generation is taking their

place. It's the one the media and the advertising industries call gen X, and they couldn't be more different from the men and women who preceded them. Where the baby boomers have voice mail, gen X has instant messaging on the Internet. Where Boomers gave out phone numbers, Xers give everyone their e-mail address. They are a new generation with new approaches to communication, information gathering, and problem-solving.

Does this mean the next generation of church will be entirely run through an electronic pipeline into the congregation's bedrooms? Not likely. Although the new generation accepts technology as a communication tool, an information resource, and an entertainment venue, they still socialize. This is a generation invested in group events—dining out, playing sports, and going to the mall. This group social interaction continues after they get married and start families. The new-generation families are gathering at parks, attending concerts, and going to sporting events with a circle of friends. To accommodate that development, Saddleback is considering replacing its row seating arrangement with tables surrounded by chairs to encourage group interactions.

A sobering statistic for new paradigm churches like Saddleback is that the average new church stops growing after about twenty-five years. The Church Growth Movement churches are now twenty-five to thirty years old. Are they about to stagnate? One professor specializing in church growth, Eddie Gibbs from the Fuller Theological Seminary, makes the point that "When a church reaches a certain size, it has to write a new plan for itself." In the business community, the buzzword is "re-engineer." We said before that Saddleback was willing to evolve to stay alive. Now's it's actually having to put the plan into action.

The New Evangelist

We have an idea of what direction mega churches will take in the future. But the question remains: who will be the next great *leader* of the Christian evangelists? For an answer, we turn to an article by Cathy Lynn Grossman in *USA Today* (June 24, 2004). Grossman draws a portrait of a person she calls a "well-disguised evangelist." His name is Cameron Strang. At twenty-eight years old, he is symbolic of the new "emerging church." Strang and other emerging leaders are different than older Christians, and those differences go beyond the three silver hoops in Strang's ears. What is new about them is their explosive brand of faith that leads them to retailers, publishers, and even churches—everything the Church Growth Movement grew up with. Strang doesn't care about politics and power plays over who will control the church, arguments that deteriorate into squabbles over denomination language and organizational red tape. To these young Christians, "God is God and Truth is Truth," none of which has a bureaucratic label.

In many ways, these are the same forces that started the Church Growth Movement. But, like everything else, the new leaders are evolving. And they might be evolving back to pre-CGM ideals. Dan Kimball, a forty-two-year-old pastor of the Vintage Faith Church in Santa Cruz, California, is the author of *The Emerging Church*. In it, Kimball insists that today's young Christians are not happy with their church opportunities and rituals. He says, "These dissatisfied young worshippers find that the mega-churches feel like Wal-Mart, that the pastors sound like Tony Robbins with some Bible verses, and the music is like a pep rally. They want to know 'Where are the crosses? Where's the expression of spirituality?'"

Interesting concept, isn't it? Are these new evangelists looking for a return to the white steeple churches? More traditional services and music? Less multimedia? Those are questions that Rick and his Saddleback ministry are going to have to answer.

Evolution

In his book, Dan Kimball talks about the changing church landscape. He cites another author, Brian McClure, who noted that most of the great cathedrals of ancient Europe were built for eager congregations. Today, they sit vacant except for the flashbulb-popping tourists taking pictures of the architecture, without pausing a second to ponder the fate of the congregations that built the churches.

Kimball uses that dramatic example to illustrate the need for seeker-sensitive churches, to avoid losing the next generation by continuing to be flexible and adjusting to changing times and needs—just the task that Rick Warren and his Saddleback brethren are trying to do. In fact, Rick endorsed Kimball's book, saying it is a "wonderful detailed example of what Purpose-Driven church can look like in a postmodern world. You need to pay attention to him [Kimball] because the times are changing."

Christian public opinion researcher George Barna of the Barna Research Group provides his insights into how the churches of tomorrow can survive through his surveys and newest book, *Think Like Jesus: Make the Right Decision Every Time*. His most surprising recent finding is that pastors are taking young children a lot more seriously than they used to. Often, pastors see children only as adjuncts of their parents; they're ignored or treated like tagalongs of the adults. As a result, Barna says, "There are thirty to thirty-five Bible stories and characters that the typical church will make sure kids are exposed to. Then they beat those stories to death year after year." Barna emphasizes the idea that adults—parents and pastors—need to connect to children better, so kids feel good about church and want to come back. He says this is important because a person's moral and spiritual foundation is virtually set by age nine.

One of the reasons children are neglected may be that there is confusion and contradiction over how to define a "successful" church. Is success measured in numbers? By how many programs or how much money a church takes in? These are measuring criteria for some churches, including the New Age mega churches. Barna makes his view clear when he says, "Jesus didn't die on the cross just so we could fill up buildings. He died so people's lives could be changed, so they would be more like Him, more like God, and live a more holy and proper way."

What concerns Barna most is that the clergy are blissfully ignorant of the situation. "What they talk about much of the time," he says, "are programs, number of members, buildings, and money—not how members' lives were changed through Christianity."

This had led him to conclude that the future of the

Christian Church is in today's teenagers, whom he calls "mosaics." In his mind, these mosaics are not like any previous generation—they have a new eclectic, nonlinear way of thinking. Barna differentiates between mosaics and the generations that preceded them in a way that explains the present church leadership's reluctance when it comes to coping with the youngest generation. He says, "As Boomers turn to plastic surgeons, miracle medicines, and postmodern philosophy to deny their age, and Busters continue to whine that they never had their due—the Mosaics are struggling to claw their way onto the main stage of cultural significance." Nevertheless, he says, 66 percent of mosaics put rapport with God way ahead of a wonderful job or great sex. This is probably not where their parents would have rated these things. Mosaics see that many parents have made a mess of their own lives; they understand that the reason adults don't talk to their children about spiritual concerns is that those parents don't know what to say.

Barna's point is that if churches are to continue to grow, a new kind of church leadership will have to emerge that can reach out and connect with preteens. Only time will tell if Rick Warren's prolific Saddleback ministry is up to the task. But if we are to take its short history as precedent, the answer will most likely be yes.

CHAPTER SEVEN

PURPOSE-DRIVEN

"The man without a purpose is like a ship without a rudder—a waif, a nothing, a no man."

—Thomas Carlyle

W HEN Rick Warren moved to Orange County with his family and started the Saddleback Valley Community Church, he knew what his purpose was: to create a religious community that would extend beyond the established limits of the Christian population to reach "the unchurched." But beyond his general goal of spreading Christianity, his plan had yet to take a concrete form. How exactly would he go about creating his ministry? How would he ensure that his church would become a part of the larger Church Growth Movement?

As it turned out, Rick's experiences in his first few years at Saddleback gave root to and solidified his evangelical mission. His nascent idea of purpose evolved into the plan that would become the driving force behind the Saddleback ministry and Rick's best-selling book, *The Purpose-Driven Life*. The purpose that had once been his alone would quickly become the purpose of more than sixteen thousand congregants and millions of readers worldwide.

Early Struggles

The need for more clearly defined answers first came in 1980, the year that Rick moved to Southern California and started Saddleback. With the help of Reverend Robert Schuller in nearby Garden Grove, other area churches, and some volunteers, the Warrens managed to start doing services in rented classrooms and other places. But being the leader of his own church was a lot harder than Rick Warren had anticipated. He had a dream, but for the time being, it wasn't enough to keep him going.

Seeing the mountaintop and imagining the view is one thing. Ascending it is an entirely different story. Rick Warren had placed himself at the foot of a tall mountain with a beautiful view. A *very* tall mountain. As is the case with many ventures, what starts out as a beautiful vision turns into harsh reality when the first blizzard hits and there isn't a blanket to be found.

As Rick started his ascent, it seemed he was going

nowhere. Keeping the 150 to 200 worshipers in the fold, paying bills, reaching out to the community, and scrambling for rented space was wearing thin on Rick. The stress must have been overwhelming at times. But Rick Warren knew one sure way to help him overcome his problems: the Bible. That was the path his parents had showed him, the one that had guided him faithfully thus far. So in the midst of all his troubles, Rick turned once more to Scripture. By praying and studying, he started to compile meaningful passages for himself, his family, and his mission. In time he concluded that he needed a blueprint for himself and for his church: a plan for living a life with purpose. And thus, his ardent desire to reach out to the unchurched began to crystallize into a life plan for both Warren and his ministry.

At the heart of Rick's mission was a special kind of evangelism: a positive, more inclusive way to spread the "good news" of Christ to both believers and nonbelievers. An excited and emboldened Rick Warren started to implement his ideas at Saddleback. In years to come, people all over the country were listening.

Even as his popularity was blossoming, the pastor was careful to share his plan in a dignified way that avoided sensationalism. Aware of the pitfalls that fame had brought to TV evangelists like Jimmy Swaggart and Jim Bakker, Rick eschewed the television route in favor of more natural settings for sharing his ideas. He knew that it would defeat his purpose to become a celebrity, and he chose to live a modest and honorable Christian life. He was interested in promoting Jesus, not himself, and that remains true today.

Fueled by his passion for evangelism, Rick developed his ministry by focusing on what was most important. He guided himself, his life, and his work by the thing that mattered most—God—and tuned out the rest. He was driven, as he once said, "by purpose and not pressure."

Eventually, his plan evolved into two acclaimed books: *The Purpose-Driven Church* is a guide for pastors that deals with how to create a popular church and gather new believers. Critics and friends alike have dubbed it a "marketing strategy" book for Christian leaders. The more popular book is *The Purpose-Driven Life*, which to date has sold over 20 million copies worldwide. It is the ultimate evolution of Rick Warren's conception of purpose for Christians, and has become the centerpiece of his Saddleback ministry.

The Anti-Self-Help Book

The Purpose-Driven Life opens with the now famous admonition "It's not about you." Rick Warren means to say that the solution to life problems doesn't come from within us. To give purpose to our lives, we must look outside of ourselves to our Creator, God. At the heart of the book is the idea that once an individual invites God to take the wheel and devotes his or her life to learning how to best serve Him, life becomes full and rewarding.

From his experience as a pastor, Rick knew that the majority of people are governed by negative feelings: guilt, resentment, anger, fear, materialism, and the need for approval from others. But he makes a point of telling his readers that they are not beholden to their past lives, and that truth can open great opportunities for their futures with God. At the center of that truth is the realization that we are not made for ourselves, but rather for God; the purpose of our lives is not to make ourselves happy, but rather to make God happy. That is why people call *The Purpose-Driven Life* the "anti-self-help book." However, by making God happy, people actually live a more fulfilled life, making themselves happy in the process.

Rick Warren wants people to discover their purpose, for it is through purpose that the Christian mission becomes less stressful, and thus more enjoyable. The best benefit of discovering purpose is that the odds of actually achieving the goal of evangelism are greatly increased.

Rick breaks his 334-page opus into six sections that guide the readers along as they discover their missions in life. The first section revolves around the question "What on Earth am I here for?" Rick develops his answers to that riddle over the next five sections, which outline a Christian's five life purposes. The reader learns that he or she:

1. Was planned for God's pleasure

2. Was formed for God's family

3. Was created to be like Christ

4. Was shaped for serving God

5. Was made for a mission

To make sure that the reader fully understands all of these purposes and their implications, Warren breaks the book down into forty smaller sections (forty days), each devoted to thinking about one aspect of the greater purpose at hand. He asks readers to cover one short chapter a day, forcing them to really take the time to ponder each lesson.

Rick goes on to ask for the reader to devote time and discussion to each of the thought-provoking questions that he provides at the end of every chapter. The questions are specifically designed to help readers shift their mind-sets and start giving themselves more fully to God. For example, one question in the fourth week of study is "What is one area where I need to stop thinking *my* way and start thinking God's way?"

Before they dip into the first chapter, however, the readers are asked to sign a covenant with Rick Warren to devote forty continuous days to *The Purpose-Driven Life*. Rather than simply reading the book, he wants them to commit to a forty-day program of study. The covenant also urges people to study the book in conjunction with other readers, whether in pairs or in more formal, small, church-based groups. No one has to—or should—take the journey alone.

Forty Days of Purpose

Week 1 of the program (days 1–6) is devoted to thinking about the question "What on Earth am I here for?" For Rick, the key to understanding the answer is realizing that life on Earth is temporary. Once the reader realizes that life on Earth is only a breath of time compared to the eternity that follows, he or she will see that his or her trials and tribulations are ephemeral. In fact, Rick says, as a Christian, it's natural not to feel completely content here.

Even though He predetermined every event in our lives, God is constantly testing us, just as he did Adam and Eve. On a smaller scale, Rick asserts that God watches how people handle their day-to-day affairs. He sees both their acts of kindness and generosity and their acts of selfishness, thereby determining how well He can trust them with His spiritual blessings. Warren illustrates his point by quoting

Luke (16:10, NLT): "Unless you are faithful in small matters, you won't be faithful in large ones."

Rick maintains that we can lead simpler and holier lives if we have the peace of mind that comes from knowing God is in control. He sees those who pursue earthly wealth as chasing an empty goal. Instead, he says, we should be preparing ourselves for eternity by striving to re-create ourselves in the image of Christ.

Week 2 of the program (days 8–14) presents the first of Rick's five purposes: "You were planned for God's pleasure." Rick asserts that God takes pleasure from our worship of Him. He asks that readers think about surrendering completely to God by making Him the center of their lives. Part of that task is to keep in constant contact with God through prayer. Rick believes it is absolutely necessary that we speak to God every day and that we meditate on His word, as manifested in the Bible. He suggests that, when you pray, you are speaking to God. Conversely, when you meditate, you are giving God a chance to speak to you.

One of the most powerful aspects of Rick Warren's plan, as he presents it in this section of the book, is that he doesn't choose any one style of prayer or worship over another. God always hears a sincere voice calling to Him. For that reason, Rick applauds the use of nontraditional music in his church. His worship music includes jazz and rock, country and soul, ballads, R & B—whatever helps him connect with worshipers. He sees no need to cling to the old familiar organ-backed hymns and denies that there is any kind of music that is distinctively "Christian."

At the end of Week 2, having exhorted his readers to communicate with God as much as possible and in whatever way they can, Rick cautions them about experiencing dry spells. He says that there will be times when it feels like we cannot get through to God in prayer. Even though we may feel frustrated, we must remember that He is always present. Feelings of despair and abandonment are just some of God's tests. If we have faith, we will overcome whatever trials we may face.

At the start of *Week 3* (days 15–21), Rick puts forth his second purpose: "You were formed from God's family." God created humans to be members of His family, and sent Jesus to Earth to help them learn to be the kind of Christians He expects them to be. As Rick says, when we place our faith in Jesus Christ, God becomes our Father, we become His children, and other believers from the past, present, and future become our brothers and sisters; the Church becomes our spiritual family. But there's one catch: although God creates us all, we don't immediately become a part of His spiritual family. We must have a second birth through baptism to truly become children of God. Rick says that baptism is not an option for Christians: it is a must.

The entire Bible, Rick reminds the reader, tells the story

of God building a family who will love and honor Him and reign with Him for eternity. For that reason, He wants believers to be in close, regular contact with other Christians. The purpose of life is learning to love both God and His people: to honor both the Father and His holy family, the church. Life without that kind of love is worthless.

Rick goes on to say that being a part of a church is a necessary component of living a healthy and holy life. A church helps us focus on God, its fellowship helps us face life's problems, its discipleship helps fortify our faith, its ministry helps fuel our talents, and its evangelism helps develop our mission. In addition, Rick believes that membership in a church is an important way of keeping Christians safe from evil. He says that those beyond the fellowship of other churchgoers and out of the reach of preachers are easy prey for Satan. The point to consider is the saying "I don't just believe, I belong."

The word "fellowship" is the focus of the third week of study in *The Purpose-Driven Life*. It's important to understand just what the term means in the context of the book and of the Saddleback ministry, because the concept of fellowship goes to the heart of Rick Warren's evangelical mission. Traditionally, fellowship means "shared experience." Although for many it may stand for chit-chat and a cup of coffee after services, according to Rick it should signify much more than being a church member and faithful attendee. True fellowship emerges out of the formation of small groups, no larger than ten, who open themselves up to honest, soul-baring discussions. In this sense, Rick follows the lead of Gilbert Bilezikian and Bill Hybels.

He maintains that true fellowship means trusting one another enough to risk hurt and humiliation by being completely open, but knowing that your brothers and sisters won't judge you. Warren goes on to say that, while Christians can experience true fellowship at various levels—by sharing conversation, studying the Bible together, or serving on mission trips or errands of mercy—the deepest kind is the fellowship of suffering. Many of the questions that Warren poses in this week of reading are specific to this area of shared suffering, based on a verse from Galatians (6:2, NLT): "Share each other's troubles and problems, and in this way obey the law of Christ."

Brothers and sisters in fellowship have not only the responsibility to reach out to other Christians when they see them struggling with a problem (even at the risk of incurring their anger), but also the task of mending broken fellowships within the church whenever they see them. Warren calls these small fellowship groups "cells," and likens them to cells in the body of Christ. Just as our body parts work together to keep us alive physically, so these small groups work together to keep the larger church alive.

The church family moves Christians out of isolation

and keeps them accountable for doing their share of God's work. Working together toward a common good—the glory of God—fuels the stability of God's family. That is the crux of the message that Rick sends to nonbelievers searching for meaning in life. He offers them the promise of inclusion and fulfillment in exchange for a complete commitment to God and His community.

In *Week 4* (days 22–28), the purpose for the reader to ponder is "You were created to become like Christ." The Bible says that all people, not just believers, possess part of the image of God. But Christians must also strive to create in themselves godly habits. We can think and reason, give and receive, love, and tell right from wrong, which makes us accountable to God, but we also must cultivate our faith by surrendering our authority to God and the Bible as Jesus did. Although Christians often mistakenly interpret Jesus' promise of abundant life to mean happiness and good health on Earth, Rick cautions us that God's ultimate goal for our lives on Earth is not comfort, but rather spiritual development.

Rick tells the reader that when you take the first step of faith, God begins to work through you, even though the change in you may at first be subtle. He refers to Ephesians to describe how the transformation should happen. A Christian must let go of old ways of acting, let the Spirit change old ways of thinking, and develop new habits in the spirit of Christ. Rick says that a person's character is the sum of his or her habits, so he asks readers to "grow up" and make sure that their deeds are consistent with their creed, and that they back up their beliefs with Christian behavior. He advises people to not merely read the Bible, but believe and live as it teaches.

This shift to leading a Christ-like life takes time and concerted effort, and it will undoubtedly be filled with temptations. But Rick reminds us that there is a purpose behind every pitfall in life—they are all part of God's plan for each of His children. He asks the reader to consider the idea that every temptation is an opportunity to advance one's faith because it offers a choice. In any situation, humans have the power to elect to do the right or the wrong thing. Unfortunately, many people just become bitter when they have to deal with problems, rather than attempt to solve them as Jesus would. These people never "grow up" in the spiritual sense.

One of the most interesting things about this fourth week of study is that to Rick Warren "growing up" means learning how to ask for help. He says that when confronted by a temptation, one should send God an SOS. He says, "To help the sinner avoid temptation, God has a 24-hour hotline in prayer," that believers should never be afraid to call, even for the same old recurring weakness. To add emphasis to his point, Rick quotes Martin Luther: "My temptations have been my masters in divinity." As long as we know where to call for help, we will be strong enough to withstand any temptation that we encounter.

At the start of *Week 5* of the program (days 29–35), Rick asks the reader to consider the purpose "You were shaped for serving God." Having chosen to follow the teachings of Jesus, Christians need to accept their assignments on Earth to make real contributions to the holy family.

Rick introduces the SHAPE acronym to illustrate his point: Christians should serve God with Spiritual gifts, Heart, Abilities, Personality, and Experiences. The key to this idea is losing the desire to better your own life and devoting yourself to the service of others. Warren reminds us that the Bible says that we should act whenever we have the opportunity to do what is right, especially for the family of believers, even when acting means risking our own happiness.

God made humans as individual as He made snowflakes, and once we accept that we are His servants, He expects us to serve Him in our own unique ways. "You were put on Earth to make contributions," Rick Warren writes; every Christian, not just ministers, monks, and nuns, is expected to participate. "A non-serving Christian is a contradiction in terms," Rick insists. No matter what your particular talent or skill is, it can and should be used in the service of the Church. Even our flaws can be turned into tools of God, if others can learn from them.

In this week, Warren once again hammers home the point that Christians devoted to serving God shouldn't worry about accumulating personal wealth. He speaks of Kingdom Builders and Wealth Builders. Both have business expertise, but while the latter group makes money for itself, Kingdom Builders make money in order to give it away. Saddleback Church is blessed with a number of business executives in its congregation who are working to make as much as they can to further the Kingdom of God. Warren encourages readers to start Kingdom Builder groups in their own churches.

Week 6, the final week of *The Purpose-Driven Life*'s forty-day program (days 36–40) centers on the most important of the five purposes for Rick Warren: "You were made for a mission." Readers learn it is their duty as a believer to be witnesses for Christ, and to share their experiences with others in order to bring them into the church. Rick explains that the Christian mission is a continuation of Jesus' mission on Earth, and that it is the duty of every believer to evangelize. He doesn't mean to imply that every Christian should quit his or her job and become a preacher, but rather that every Christian has the responsibility of sharing the news of Jesus with others wherever he or she goes. In these last (and longest) chapters, Rick shows readers practical ways to spread the Gospel.

For Rick Warren, this most sacred purpose is closely linked to the influence of his father, Jimmy Warren, who was a minister for fifty years. As he lay on his deathbed, Jimmy kept repeating, "Got to save one more for Jesus, got to save one more for Jesus." The scene is still vivid in Rick's mind, and he says that his father's words motivate him every day. He urges his readers, and all Christians, to ponder the idea that God wants to use each and every one of them to say something about Christ to the world.

At the conclusion of *The Purpose-Driven Life*, readers are left with the message that "God wants us to introduce people to Christ, bring them into His fellowship, help them grow to maturity and discover their place of service, and then send them out to reach others." With those words, Rick Warren sums up the essence of *The Purpose-Driven Life*. He also describes the personal life plan that is a product of his own difficult journey as a pastor. Over time, Warren was able to develop his own clearly defined purpose: to reach out to the unchurched, to find every man and woman still searching for a source of meaning in life, and to bring them into the Christian family. That Christian evangelism is the heart and soul of Warren's ministry at Saddleback Church.

The Purpose-Driven Phenomenon

The Purpose-Driven Church, and to a greater extent, *The Purpose-Driven Life* put Rick Warren and his ministry on the fast track. Saddleback Valley Community Church went from 150 to 200 members listening to services wherever the church could rent space, to a 16,000-member congregation in a church that sits on more than 120 acres of land.

Saddleback is now one of the most prosperous mega churches in America. Warren has been able to expand his ministry to include programs that deal not only with religion, but also with important issues like martial trouble, living with the elderly and handicapped, addiction, unwed motherhood, terminal illness, teen depression, and more.

Embracing the philosophy of Norman Vincent Peale and others who merged religion and psychology, Warren has taken advantage of the success of his purpose-driven ministry by having the church itself provide these important counseling resources to whoever needs them. Some critics are put off by this no-holds-barred tactic of bringing people (physically and emotionally) into the church. But others see Rick Warren, bolstered by the fantastic popularity of *The Purpose-Driven Life*, as the leader of the next generation of evangelical preachers—the heir to the legacies of Peale, Billy Graham, and Robert Schuller.

The 40 Days of Purpose program set forth by *The Purpose-Driven Life* has had prolific success around the world, touching the lives of hundreds of thousands of people. In the fall of 2004 alone, more than 2,800 churches of all denominations across the country signed up to take part in one of Rick Warren's quarterly 40 Days of Purpose campaigns (in which entire congregations read *The Purpose-Driven Life* together and undertake the forty-day program in concert with Saddleback Church).

One woman named Jane, a Lutheran by upbringing, but now attending another community church in Orange County, said that several small groups at her church bought Rick Warren's book and went through the forty-day program as directed. "He introduced the course with a video, and was really mesmerizing," she said. When asked if she felt it was helpful in her life, she said, "Oh, yes, we all got a lot out of it. It's best to study in small groups because then you can all have a chance to participate in the discussion."

"I think the part about relationships had the most meaning for me," Jane said thoughtfully. "I'm kind of shy, and it makes people think I am standoffish, which I'm not. But it's hard to get down to discussing personal things because of pride. The forty-day program helped me overcome that."

Many different Christian denominations have participated in the forty-day program, reflecting the inclusive appeal of Rick Warren's brand of evangelism, which is woven into *The Purpose-Driven Life*. One of the book's obvious gestures of inclusion is the fact that the nearly one thousand scripture verses quoted by Rick come from more than a dozen versions of the Bible. He points out that the Bible was originally written in roughly eleven thousand Hebrew, Aramaic, and Greek words. However, a typical English version uses only about six thousand words. Each translation chooses to focus on certain nuances and meanings while eliminating others. By using different translations, Rick hopes to bring the reader as close as he can to God's original words.

One specific area in which the forty-day program has had a noticeable effect is in prison reform. Saddleback Church donates materials to any prison that agrees to incorporate the plan into its rehabilitation regime. The results of this prison outreach have been nothing short of spectacular. Hector Lozano says that before the program was introduced to the Jamestown Sierra Conservation Prison in California, "We couldn't go more than two weeks without a riot or a lockdown or one prison gang attacking another gang."

In one year, he counted 5 riots, 103 violent incidents, 4 assaults on members of the prison staff, and 5 lockdowns. But in the year following the implementation of the program, there were only 67 violent incidents and only 1 lockdown. "It took off like wildfire, with inmates going cell to cell to recruit participants," another prison spokesperson recalled. He also noted that the inmates had taken it upon themselves to create a neutral "holy ground" in the prison yard where Christians and non-Christians alike could pray.

Rick Warren visited Jamestown Prison personally in August of 2003. When he arrived, Lozano expressed dismay that the prison couldn't pay Warren back for all of the Bibles, books, study materials, and videos that Saddleback had donated. Rick pointed out that the prisoners turning toward God instead of violence was fair payment.

On an even larger scale, another consensus-building concept that Rick puts forth in *The Purpose-Driven Life* is the importance of peacemaking. He reminds us that it was God who selected our different personalities, races, backgrounds, and preferences, and that we should enjoy rather than just tolerate our differences. Neither the Christian Church nor the world will ever be trouble-free. The sooner that idea is grasped and we admit that we all need God's grace to survive, the better off we'll be. Different races and ethnicities therefore should not be tolerated—they should be *accepted*, because in accepting God, we accept what He has created.

In Rick Warren's ministry, peacemaking is important on every level, from getting a pair of squabbling neighbors back on speaking terms, to encouraging dialogue between countries violently opposed to each other's view of the world. Although Rick speaks primarily of the need to mend relationships within the church family, through honest, loving effort, his philosophy also holds on the international level.

Changing the Face of Evangelism

There can be no doubt that *The Purpose-Driven Life* and Rick Warren's Saddleback ministry have had a ripple effect across the entire planet. Missionaries from Rick's church have helped build hundreds of churches worldwide. On a grander scale, Rick has changed the way pastors around the globe think about the process of bringing nonbelievers to the church. Lee Powell, assistant pastor of the 2,500-member Branch Creek Community Church in Harleysville, Pennsylvania, was thrilled with the progress made by those who participated in their forty-day program. "God did a mighty work here," he said.

But not all of the responses to the Warren-inspired wave of evangelism—and more specifically, to *The Purpose-Driven Life*—have been positive. In a February 2004 article in the *Atlanta Journal-Constitution,* John Blake wrote that the answer to the question "What on Earth am I here for?" was "to buy Warren's books." Blake illustrated his criticism of the Warren ministry with the pastor's own favorite delicacy, saying that his two books "are being devoured like Krispy Kreme donuts" in Christian households.

Larry Gilbert, who runs the Church Growth Institute in Elkton, Maryland, echoed Blake's sentiment. He said that

Rick "is a master marketer who would be Lee Iacocca if he were out in the world of business." But in Gilbert's mind, all Warren has done is package Christianity in a way that makes it applicable to the average guy. Rick Warren has managed to demonstrate how religion can be useful to ordinary people whose focus tends to be on themselves and their problems, but who still feel unfulfilled.

The Purpose-Driven Life is remarkable for many reasons, but certainly one of its most amazing qualities is its incredible popularity. That fact is a testament not only to the power of Rick Warren's message, but also to his skill in spreading it. As John Blake cleverly phrased it, Warren combines "the missionary zeal of Paul with the persistence of an Amway salesman." And Blake is right: Rick's book is both the summary of and the driving force behind his evangelical ministry. It is the centerpiece of Rick Warren's effort to attract the unchurched. And all signs seem to indicate that book sales—and the ministry—will continue to grow for years to come.

CHAPTER EIGHT

THE WARREN
METHOD

THERE'S a story that often gets repeated at Saddleback Church—a tale of conversion. It goes something like this: An unchurched man or woman hears something about Rick Warren. That person could be a friend or relative of a congregation member, or someone totally new. Maybe he or she skimmed through Rick's book *The Purpose-Driven Life* and liked its message. Maybe this person wandered up the road to Saddleback once, and wondered about its beautiful and friendly environment. Whatever the reason, something about the church grabs his or her attention.

Next, this person attends a service at Saddleback, dressed not as if for a formal affair, but in comfortable clothing, as if going to a neighbor's backyard gathering. As soon as this person arrives, he or she is warmly welcomed and made to feel a part of the church community. This unchurched man or woman appreciates that the sermon is broken up into different messages delivered by several people. In between the segments, there is wonderful music.

After the service, the visitor notices a lot activity on the church grounds. People are gathering in small groups for lessons, or just to discuss their community and the church programs—programs that benefit neighborhoods, help people battle addictions, or send aid to people in faraway places. There are so many choices of programs that the visitor is sure several could use his or her skills or expertise.

This curious unchurched person starts attending Saddleback regularly to hear more of Rick Warren's message, the message that is fixing the bumps in his or her road of life. For the first time, this person begins to see purpose in his or her existence. The unchurched person accepts Jesus Christ as his or her Savior and is baptized at Saddleback Valley Community Church.

These kinds of conversions occur at the rate of over one thousand a year at Saddleback Church. In the world of Christian evangelism, that number is nothing short of phenomenal. Rick's fantastic success as an evangelist is, without a doubt, linked to *The Purpose-Driven Life* and the popularity of his forty-day program. But for newcomers to Saddleback, the book is only the beginning. The next step is actually becoming an active member of the church. To achieve this goal—to help prospective members along in their journeys—Rick offers programs that serve as guidebooks for membership. He describes these programs using two simple geometric shapes: diamonds and circles.

Fishing for Men with Diamonds

Throughout history, Christians have used symbols to represent their faith. We've all probably seen the metallic fish stuck to the trunks of cars on the highway. The fish symbol evolved as a secret way of referring to Jesus. (The first letters of the five words "Jesus Christ, Son of God, Savior" in Greek spell "fish.") Today Warren's diamond symbol stems from a more contemporary American language: baseball. Visualize a baseball diamond with four bases: first, second, third, and home, plus a pitcher's mound. That diamond is the foundation of Warren's CLASS program. The goal of the **Christian Life And Service Seminar** is to not only educate people about the Saddleback ministry and what it stands for, but also convince them to commit their lives to its purpose and growth.

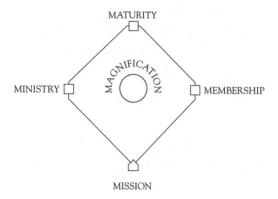

The CLASS program has four levels corresponding to the four bases of a baseball diamond. Each of the first three bases represents getting one step closer to home plate, which symbolizes becoming an active missionary on behalf of Saddleback Church. Together, the four bases and the pitcher's mound correspond to the five purposes of the church, as Warren conceives of them: to *connect*, to *grow*, to *serve*, to *share*, and to *worship*. To make those five purposes even easier to remember in the context of the program, Warren frames them in terms of the five Ms: Membership, Maturity, Ministry, Mission, and Magnification.

Class 101

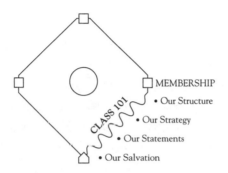

MEMBERSHIP
- Our Structure
- Our Strategy
- Our Statements
- Our Salvation

Class 101—the path to the first base of Membership—is open to everyone, even people who aren't sure they want to join Saddleback. The bulk of the class consists of general information about the church, its background, and its plans for the future. It is split into four informational sessions: Our Salvation, Our Statements, Our Strategy, and Our Structure.

Right from the start, Class 101 makes it clear that belonging to Saddleback means more than just showing up for services: every Saddleback member, in Rick's mind, must be devoted to the mission of evangelism. But while the class doesn't hide the fact that joining the church means making a serious commitment, neither does it insist that people decide then and there. If people aren't sure they want to join the church by the end of 101, they can leave with no strings attached. In fact, if they know Saddleback definitely isn't right, the staff will help guide them to another place of worship that better suits them.

If people are willing to open their lives to God and accept Jesus as their Savior, the entry fee to the realm of salvation is doing God's Work. The expectations of the commitment to serve the Lord are laid out in the beginning so that there are no surprises later. Warren does not want people committing to Saddleback for the wrong reasons, or looking back and feeling like they were coerced into the decision.

If a person does make the commitment to become a part of Saddleback, the next step is to fill out a membership application that admits the person to the membership program. People must have completed Class 101, been baptized, and signed a covenant of commitment to Christ and the church to officially reach the level of membership—first base in Warren's diamond scenario.

This person is now ready to move on the path to second base: Maturity.

Class 201

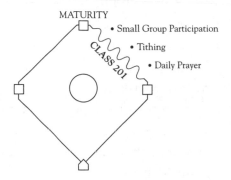

Class 201 is the pathway to maturity. In it, members work on making God a part of their daily lives. Reaching Maturity involves three components. The first is to commit daily to speaking to God through private, reflective prayer—speaking to Him and asking for continued guidance. This habit should become a daily reflection on the individual's relationship with God, church, and the community.

The second component of Maturity is financial support of God's work through tithing. The purpose of the tithing is twofold: it serves as a reminder of the self-sacrifice of doing God's work, especially in today's material world, and it also drives home the point that commitment to God reaches into every area of life, even into the professional, money-making sphere.

The third part of Maturity is to become a member of one of the hundreds of small groups within the church. This component integrates a new member with people who have already taken the journey, and gives him or her the chance to begin true fellowship with other believers. All three aspects of the journey to Maturity—daily prayer, tithing, and small group participation—give a person the tools, the system, and the encouragement he or she needs to do the Lord's work, and prepares that person for the next objective: the third base of Ministry.

Class 301

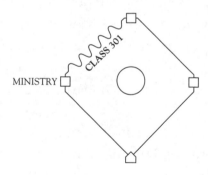

Class 301 is the pathway to Ministry, in which members dedicate themselves to participating actively at Saddleback.

In Rick Warren's mind, all people who accept Jesus Christ are ministers of His work—not just those people who speak from the pulpit. Class 301 is meant to make the point that being committed to the Lord is a full-time job for every believer. How someone behaves in public is a reflection on his or her ministry as well as on the Saddleback Valley Community Church. Ministry is a spiritual uniform for the believer, but instead of just wearing it, the believer must live it.

In Class 301, every member signs up for one of Saddleback's dozens of thriving organized church ministries. Before joining, members are subject to an interview process to ensure that they're placed properly. The interview measures the depth of commitment the person is ready to make; it also brings to light the best talents he or she has to offer. Everyone is born with gifts from God to do His work, and the interview process helps the person figure out what those gifts truly are, whether it be public speaking, writing, singing or preaching.

Class 401

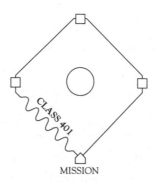

MISSION

Class 401 is final step of the journey: the pathway to Mission, represented by home plate. It is in this final stage that members join in the cause of evangelism. Rick Warren always believed that he would build a church for the unchurched, but he also knew that after bringing them home, he would send them back out into the world to find more lost sheep. The goal of Rick's ministry is not baptism—that just gets people to show up to church. Rather, the goal is evangelism—people spreading the Good News of Jesus far and wide. And what better people to have as evangelists than those who converted later in life? Those who know what it's like to be lost, and where to find people who are seeking.

The Pitcher's Mound

The glue that binds the four-base process together is magnification, represented by the pitcher's mound. Just as a pitcher's pitches are the fuel for runs in a baseball game—the source of the hits that push a player around the bases to home—magnification, or worship and praise of the Lord, is the fuel for a person's journey to Mission. Group worship, private prayer, ministry, and community evangelism are all bound together by magnification.

Behind Rick Warren's CLASS program and its familiar baseball symbolism is the idea that a simple, understandable course will make the process of conversion more comfortable for unbelievers, allowing them to move seamlessly from one stage of commitment to the next. It's purpose is to help Rick connect more genuinely with people as he tries to make them part of the church's world. He doesn't want to scare people away with fire-and-brimstone warnings about Hell and the wrath of God; he wants to include them in the spirit of Christ's love. The CLASS program is the perfect kind of loving, individualized program Rick needs to help seekers round the four bases of membership, maturity, ministry, and finally mission. As he likes to say, "You don't get credit for people left on base!"

Circles of Faith

The second symbol that plays an important role in Rick's ministry is composed of five concentric circles. These circles have a strong relationship to the bases in the CLASS program.

Once again, Warren uses alliteration to describe the components of this big-picture metaphor: from outermost to innermost, the circles represent the Community, the Crowd, the Congregation, the Committed, and finally the Core.

The Community

The largest outside circle, the Community, refers to the world of people beyond the church. Rick tries to stir up interest in Saddleback in this group of people—they are the primary targets of his evangelism. Members of the community might be curious about the church's attractive physical facilities, community image, service and counseling programs, or maybe just the mobs of people who already attend. Rick's goal is to convince members of the community to start attending services.

The Crowd

The next circle inward is the Crowd. These are the people who attend Saddleback regularly and are genuinely interested in the Good News of Christ. Many individuals in the Crowd will sign up for Class 101 on the way to Membership. The design of the church, the numerous welcoming committees and small groups, and even the messages of the sermons themselves are geared toward this group.

The Congregation

The next circle in, the Congregation, is composed of those who have embraced the teachings of Jesus and are actively committed to the church. People in the Congregation have taken Class 101 and become members of Saddleback. Many of them will enroll in Class 201 on their way to the second base of Maturity, where reflective prayer and group interaction will further build their knowledge, love, and commitment to the Lord.

The Committed

The fourth circle is populated by the Committed. These are people who have become mature in their faith (have rounded second base), and are on their way to the third base of Ministry. The Committed have made a choice to serve Christ. Their task is to determine which of their unique talents best serve God.

The Core

People in the innermost circle are known as the Core. Members of the Core have passed third base, reached the home plate of mission, and committed themselves to the purpose of Saddleback Church as a whole: evangelism. Unlike a core group in business or politics—composed of a few select people, a number which never grows in membership—Rick Warren's Core constantly feeds back into the four circles that precede it. Core members are the driving force behind pulling in more people from the community. When we think of it that way, we can visualize Rick's circle diagram dynamically but in reverse, where the Core is a pebble that strikes water and radiates out toward the surrounding area.

Both Rick's diamond-based CLASS program and his circle symbol share a common goal: bringing unbelievers to Christ and dedicating them to the cause of evangelism. According to Rick Warren, it's not enough just to baptize new believers; churches need to get their members to commit to evangelism. And that message doesn't just apply to Saddleback. In Rick's mind, it holds for every Christian church in the world.

Part of what has made the CLASS program so effective in churches outside of Saddleback is Rick's insight into the needs and nuances of different congregations. People bring all sorts of varied experiences to church. Rick understands that his programs need to be adapted to particular circumstances in order to be effective. He gives seminars for pastors specifically geared toward that goal, and professes to be overjoyed when, for example, some church leaders turn the CLASS baseball diamond into a basketball court, or a ladder, or even the likeness of a tree, depending on what "bases" they feel they need to emphasize most in their congregation.

Rick has called the five Saddleback purposes (connect, grow, serve, share, worship) as the "Intel chip" of the Christian Church. What he means is, in the same way that wildly different computer systems operate using the same electronic building blocks, different churches can use the five purposes to construct an invisible framework suited to their own needs. Rick's theory about music in church is a great example of this idea. He doesn't care if city churches blast rap music from the pulpit any more than he cares about traditional parishes playing organ hymns. His hope is that, as they conform the Saddleback programs to their own congregations, pastors will gain insight into the needs of their people and therefore find more effective ways of promoting evangelism.

An Internet for God

One of the challenges Warren faced when he started Saddleback was figuring out how to evangelize to people in remote locations, as his father had. He knew that to grow as a mega church, Saddleback had to stay in one location. But how could he reach people across the sprawling Southern California area?

By the time Saddleback grew to ten thousand members, the solution had already presented itself: the Internet. Rick realized that through the Internet, he could reach not only people in remote California locations but also pastors worldwide. He created a website called Pastor.com, now said to be one of the most comprehensive private communication systems for pastors in the world. Through his website, Rick is able to provide other religious leaders with great resources.

Rick once said, "I'm a toolmaker. I believe tools can change the world." In keeping with that idea, he offers a "Ministry Toolbox" online newsletter on Pastor.com. This newsletter gives great tips on recruiting new members (evangelizing), as well as insights on balancing individual worship and discipleship, sample sermon scripts, and general ideas for improving sermon technique. His goal is to disseminate to pastors around the world his own practiced and proven method of recruiting unchurched men and women.

Rick doesn't apologize for his pragmatic approach to ministry. He's honest enough to say that he is in favor of people modifying his programs into whatever works for their particular churches—as long as they accomplish the goal of bringing the unchurched to Jesus. On a grander scale, he understands the need to demystify Christianity, to make it comprehensible to the average person. In a February 2004 issue of his "Toolbox" newsletter, Warren said, "If you want to communicate the vision for your ministry, you need to compare it to something everybody already relates to. How many times did Jesus say in the New Testament, 'The kingdom of Heaven is like . . .'? And then He would give an analogy, a parable, or a metaphor?" All the evidence suggests that Rick Warren's diamond and circle imagery is doing just that.

A Mission of Love

Critics of Rick Warren (and the Church Growth Movement as a whole) claim that Saddleback is as much a business as it is a religious organization. Between the his use of the Internet, the success of *The Purpose-Driven Life*, and

Saddleback's seeming emphasis on membership numbers, it's understandable that some people see a corporate, rather than a biblical mind-set in Warren's ministry. A skeptical article written by William Lobdell (*Los Angeles Times*, September 19, 2003) focused on the aspects of Warren's ministry that seem excessively business-oriented: the multimillion-dollar worth of the church and the facts that Rick has copyrighted the phrase "Purpose-Driven" and created his own website.

But Rick would argue that he's merely carrying the mission of Jesus into the twenty-first century. With Pastor.com, Rick sees a way to reach people his father couldn't possibly have reached—he's just taking advantage of changing times and new technology. By evolving, Rick has been able to move his ministry ideas to the farthest corners of the world.

Another thing those critics fail to take into account is the role that Rick himself plays in the phenomenal growth of his church. Rick Warren is a truly charismatic spiritual leader. It's clear to anyone who experiences one of his Saddleback services that he truly loves what he does. He relishes standing up at the podium, looking out at the smiling crowd, and sharing the Good News of Jesus. He is devoted to his calling, even when it causes him physical pain. For years, Rick has suffered from a respiratory problem that severely limits his ability to preach—one that, at times, has caused him to collapse in front of his congregation. But he has found a way to carry on by breaking his lesson up into fifteen-minute segments and resting in between.

Rick isn't interested in the money or fame that goes along with being a high-profile figure. He avoids the media as much as he can, remarking that "The spotlight blinds you." Unlike the high-powered business executives his critics might compare him to, Rick Warren keeps almost nothing for himself.

The world, and the Christian Church, has changed a lot in the past century. The importance of maintaining different denominations has waned. The burgeoning evangelical movement reflects that the "new" Christian is moving away from labels toward a Warren-esque idea of general Christian purpose. Saddleback's pragmatic, flexible programs are designed for the new generation of collaborative pastors. Rick's use of the Internet, both through Pastors.com and in conjunction with *The Purpose-Driven Life*, is a prime example of that trend. (Pastors who participate in a 40 days of Purpose campaign can log onto Rick's website and download his daily lessons to use in their own congregations.) The official Saddleback Church website (Saddleback.com) is extremely comprehensive in its own right, offering a wealth of information for everyone from first-time visitors to members of the ministry.

Rick envisions Saddleback as a "teaching church" with not only the ability, but also the responsibility, to pass on its lessons to other congregations. "We've trained more pastors than all the seminaries combined," he says. And he's done so in classic, down-to-earth Saddleback style. Rick sometimes cites the example of Ronald Reagan, "The Great Communicator," who took care always to speak in terms that everyone could understand. Reagan once used an analogy to describe the national deficit, which at that point was around a trillion dollars: he asked his viewers to look at the small pile of one-dollar bills on his desk, and envision a stack as high as the Empire State Building.

In a similar way, Warren embraces accessible metaphors to connect with his listeners: for example, the language of baseball. He also embraces trends in popular culture, rather than shunning them. In January 2004, Warren announced to his congregation that he had leased all seven movie theaters in South Orange County for two nights in a row—a total of thirty thousand seats—with the expectation that each and every one of them would go see Mel Gibson's *The Passion*.

In the end, it's not just Rick Warren's marketing savvy that makes him so successful. It's his deep understanding of human nature, of people's needs and desires, that makes him a preacher apart. In the next chapter, we'll find out just how far his influence has spread.

CHAPTER NINE

THE P.E.A.C.E. PLAN

RICK Warren continues to amaze everyone within his sphere of influence. What would one normally expect of a man who has been at the same job in the same place for almost twenty-five years? A semiretired man figuring out what his pension will be. But not Rick Warren.

In November of 2003 he once more surprised his congregation by talking about the past and sliding immediately into a description of totally unexpected future for himself and his church.

In a call to Christian service that was surprising but also so classically characteristic of this dynamic leader, he told them that they were entering a new phase of Saddleback

Church's history. He said, "In 1980 when Saddleback was started, I was twenty five and I made a forty-year commitment to this church and thought, 'If I spend forty years in that one place, what will I do?' "

Looking back, he could answer his own question by dividing the church's life into thirds. The first portion, beginning with the founding of Saddleback in the 1980s, would be devoted to creating and nurturing the church locally there in Orange County. That has been accomplished. By the end of the 1980s, the church had grown to about six thousand members. During that first decade, Warren focused on the local situation and didn't travel much or speak anywhere else.

Then came the 1990s, and Rick decided it was time to expand onto the national scene, which meant connecting with other Christian churches across the country to help and bless them, too. In this period Saddleback grew from about six thousand members to fifteen thousand, but it also grew by helping other churches and training their leaders in the methods Rick had successfully been using at Saddleback Church.

Recently Rick dropped a bombshell on his congregation by saying, "When we came to the twenty-first century, I said, 'Okay, now we're going global and we're going to focus not just on our community, and we're going to focus not just on the nation, but *we're going to focus on being a blessing to the entire world.'* " This is the way of Rick Warren. He is still imbued with the love of Jesus and the dedication to spreading His word, just as his father, Jimmy Warren, Sr., did before him.

At the end of his talk, Warren set forth his analysis of the five biggest problems on Earth that he believes we must solve, and indeed can solve, with guidance from God.

Millions Don't Know Jesus

Rick says that there are still billions of people who have never heard the name of Jesus Christ. It's hard to believe that, twenty centuries after Jesus. Rick paraphrases Paul's words in Romans 10:14, saying, "Before the people can ask the Lord to save them, they must believe in Him. Before they can believe in Him, they must hear about Him. And for them to hear about Him, someone must tell them." Billions still have not heard.

Shortage of Leaders

Rick says that much of the world is bewildered because there is a shortage of qualified leaders. The world is in a mess because of poor leadership. The so-called "leaders" we have are full of themselves and focus only on what they and their immediate cronies want, without regard to their people. Yes, we have a lot of bosses, plenty of dictators, and a multitude of potentates, but we have very few servant leaders who think of the people they lead instead of themselves.

Rick cites the Bible (Proverbs 11:14 NLT): "Without wise leadership, a nation falls." He also cites Proverbs 16:12 (Msg.), "Sound leadership has a moral foundation."

He told the congregation that there are 2.1 million pastors in Third World countries, but 1.9 million of them have never been trained. That doesn't mean they did not have seminary training or college. It means they had no *high school*. So how can you lead somebody when you haven't been trained as an effective leader? What is the result of this lack of qualified leadership?

THE PLAGUE OF POVERTY

Over half of the world—more than 3 billion people—live on less than $2 a day. When you just think about that for a moment, that is an incredible fact—most of the people of the world subsist on under $2 a day! They have no skills, no job opportunities, no future, and no hope. They're hungry, they're homeless, and they're helpless.

WIDESPREAD ILLNESS

The alarming truth is that millions of people will die in the next week from diseases and starvation that could be prevented. That's a condition that no true Christian can ignore and not attempt to change. Rick says the Bible teaches that apathy angers God.

ILLITERACY AND IGNORANCE

In today's world, even with all of the information that is available via the Internet and other avenues of learning, half of the world is still illiterate. How are they going to get ahead? How are they going to learn about Jesus?

"So, what do we do about these problems?" asks Rick Warren. They are so big there is only one group that can handle them, he says. The one group big enough is local churches, because there are millions and millions of churches. Churches have the widest distribution system. You can go into villages overseas that don't have a clinic, don't have a school, don't have a store—but they have a church. There is no wider distribution channel than the Church of God. The church has hundreds of millions of members around the world. The church has the moral authority to handle these issues. And the church has the power of God to do it. The governments don't have the power to solve these problems.

Additionally, the Church is going to outlast political and other entities. It has been here since Jesus founded it two thousand years ago. Since then, governments have come and gone, wars have been fought, and organizations have disappeared, but the church keeps on going.

Rick Warren designs thought-provoking plans. From his earliest evangelical days planning concerts, newsletters, and worship meetings at Ukiah High School, to the founding and growth of Saddleback Church, Rick has always studied, planned, and laid out concepts, and in 2003 he outlined his grand plan to take his ministry global. Since he loves acronyms, he called his concept P.E.A.C.E.

P.E.A.C.E.

Here are the parts of Rick's global P.E.A.C.E. Plan that he is launching in the third decade of his ministry.

"P" FOR PLANT CHURCHES

The "P" stands for planting churches, because Rick says that God is in the church building business, and planting a church is the first step in combating evil. In particular, he

says that we need churches where there are none now because the most important thing for the people in a church-
less community is to have a place where they can be
introduced to Jesus Christ. That's creating something that
will be there a long time.

When Rick first introduced this concept of planting
churches, he knew some of his congregation might be skeptical. How could *they* possibly start churches in remote areas
of the world? So introduced nine people from the audience:
Alphonso, Alexis, Lydia, Cynthia, Jerry, Pat, Mike, Shiela,
and Don. This was the small group that started Saddleback
Church twenty-five years ago—a church that has become
one of the biggest churches in America. Then, he asked the
group if any of them had known anything about how to start
a church. The answer was no from everyone, including Rick
Warren! He said, "I was only twenty-five years old. And
some of these nine people were brand-new believers, and
some hadn't come to Christ yet. This was the wildest ride
we ever took. This church was not started by anybody who
knew how to do it. It was started by volunteers who just
said, 'We're people. We're a small group. Let's start a
church,' and half of us didn't even know the Lord yet."
Since then, Saddleback has "planted" thirty-six other
churches in Southern California and has helped thousands
of others get started.

Then, Rick told about a Christian bookstore that takes

its staff overseas for ten days every year to start churches and has started 131 of them. These were not pastors or mission-aries. These were just people.

"The only way we're going to help millions of people to hear the name of Jesus is to plant hundreds of churches around the world—under trees, in cars—you don't have to have a building to have a church. If anybody knows that, we do. We grew to over ten thousand before we built our first building. We met in all sorts of places and told people, 'If you can figure out where we are this week, you get to come.' "

"E" FOR EQUIP LEADERS

The "E" stands for equipping leaders to run those churches. Rick says that we need to be good leaders, and we need to train others to be good leaders. In Saddleback Church's twenty-three years, the church has realized that to keep growing, you have to pass on what you have learned. Rick cites II Timothy 2:2 (Msg.), "Pass on what you heard from me—the whole congregation saying Amen! to reliable lead-ers who are competent to teach others." As a mark of what needs to be done, he says that great numbers of Christians and many ministers overseas don't even have a Bible.

Rick Warren says that we need leaders—but what kind? Do we need more of Bill Gates, Jack Welch, and Warren

Buffett? Rick says no. Not when we already have a perfect leader in Jesus Christ. We need to learn to lead like Jesus.

Here, as he always does, Rick taps the best and the most famous to help train church leaders to be like Jesus. He has hired Ken Blanchard, author of best-selling *The One Minute Manager,* to come to Saddleback to help train people how to be effective leaders at home, in business, in school, and in church. It is a dramatic and impressive move, one that is typical of Rick Warren.

"A" FOR ASSIST THE POOR

Rick believes that God favors the poor, and that it is a test of our faith the way we treat them. He says that religion is not about saying prayers; it's about how you treat those in need. He cites a World Vision study that found there are 600 million poor in the world that could get out of poverty if someone would just loan them a little bit of money. He preaches that God blesses those who help the poor.

"C" FOR CURE THE SICK

Horribly, every day 27,000 children die from *curable* diseases! The greatest cause is unclean water, and the second is malaria, both of which are correctable. In addition, 14 million children become orphans every year due to AIDS.

Rick says that we are God's plan to cure these problems. The answer is not the government or "those people over there." The answer is you and I.

One typical project has been sending church members out with information and medical kits they call "Clinic in a Box." It's a plastic box filled with about $5,000 worth of antibiotics and malaria medicine (which costs the church about $350).

"E" FOR EDUCATION

Finally, "E" is for education: learning to train the next generation to live better, so that we stop losing these children. Warren says that none of these problems are new. What is new is the way that he wants to solve them. The way he chooses is revolutionary: not the great convocations, but small groups. He says that large, bureaucratic groups have traditionally done missionary work while boards and churches have been told to keep out. The church's role, Rick says, was, "you pay, you pray, and you stay out of the way." He and Saddleback Church are changing that to, "all go, all pray, all pay." Warren and Saddleback have already had 4,500 people go out on some mission project somewhere, such as "Clinic in a Box."

Next up are Church-in-a-Box and School-in-a-Box.

*   *   *

Reflecting on his own experience, Rick says, "All we need is the will to do it. When I was a twenty-five-year-old, and God said, 'Go to California and start a church', everybody said, 'You're nuts. You have no members, no money, no building, nothing.' I feel as confident about this as I did the day we started Saddleback Church, and look what has happened. I believe God brought you here to this church—you're not here by accident—you're not here to sit, sulk, and sour. God wants to use you and I'm coming after you. What if each of you adopt a village and do what average people can do—un-average things with extraordinary results?"

He makes his point with his Biblical reminder, "The more we are blessed by God, the more He expects us to help others. The Bible says that much is required of those to whom much is given." All of which is nothing more than the gospel that Rick Warren learned years ago at home in Ukiah.

CHAPTER TEN

PUTTING PURPOSE TO WORK

RICK Warren would be the first to admit there's more to running a mega church than a large membership. In fact, he recognizes that mega churches have to deal with a particular set of concerns that more traditional churches don't have to face. He has proven himself equally as adept at dealing with these larger, conceptual issues as at attracting unbelievers to Jesus.

To meet these challenges, Rick has a simple three-part formula for success. *First, simplify your message.* Make the journey to Jesus easy for people to understand. For example, the Diamonds and Circles diagrams with alliteration—easy to visualize and easy to remember the words. Simplicity helps in two ways. One is it shortens the time it takes for someone to "get" the idea. The second is it prevents complications that can be distractions. Distractions not only waste time, but throw the mission off course.

Another side benefit to simplifying the message is that you really have to know what you're talking about to say so much in so few words. Rick didn't come up with Purpose-Driven in a few seconds. It took him a year of prayer, soul-searching, conceptualizing, rethinking, and finally boiling everything down into one simple phrase that summed up many things.

The second of the three-part formula is to *rely on your close friends*. This doesn't just mean that close friends are on call, waiting for that inspirational moment someone needs their assistance. It means that the friendship has been nurtured over years and each person knows the plan and the role they are to play in it. These friendships also bring loyalty and respect, which make it much easier to implement large initiatives—like building a mega church.

Close friends also tend to be more candid in conversation, which is absolutely necessary to the success of any large-scale program. There are no hidden agendas with candid conversation. Additionally, new members to the organization notice the open, honest candor with which people talk to each other—and therefore feel more comfortable speaking up and offering new ideas instead themselves.

No matter what, in every profession, there are critics. Critics of the rely on your close friends approach will say that this is creating a "good old boys network." People will whisper, "Oh, so-and-so got the job because they knew Rick back when." The critics should put themselves in Rick Warren's shoes for a moment. They have this operation to set up and run. And it's a big operation—building a mega church. There is no money, so the first resource available is people. Who do they hire? People who *know* what needs to be done. People who can be *trusted* to show up and do the job. People who *won't quit* when things get tough. People who *understand* the mission. Who fits these criteria? Close friends.

Rick Warren brought a close friend, Glen Kreun, on board at Saddleback in the early years, around 1982. Kreun had just finished at the seminary and had contacted Rick. He told Rick that he was ready to do God's work anywhere in the world *except* Southern California. After more discussion—perhaps convincing is a better term—Kreun agreed to come to Saddleback to help grow Rick Warren's ministry. Twenty-two years later, Glen Kreun is still living in Southern California, as the executive pastor of Saddleback Valley Community Church.

The third component of Rick Warren's formula for success is to *stay true to your mission*. So many initiatives fail because they go off on tangents. This is also what separates the Warren ministry from most other organizations: they *know* what their mission is. Most organizations don't know what their mission is, so they meander aimlessly because they never defined their objective. Some organizations recognize this, hire an outside consultant, and force their people to spend three agonizing days writing a mission statement as though they were writing their application for the Harvard Business School. And at the end of all that, they still don't get it. Why? Because they never had to suffer as greatly and deeply as Rick Warren did at the start of Saddleback. They never had to get down so deep into their core beliefs—stripping everything else away that really didn't matter—to find out what their mission was. That's how Rick Warren was able to come up with his mission and learn to stay true to it.

Rick Warren's mission is very simple: evangelize. Everything his ministry does is based on that single objective. It makes decision-making easy and quick. This simple, single focus allows all involved to meet the challenges of today and tomorrow, so they can adapt and continue to grow.

New Challenges

What are the new challenges Rick Warren will be applying his formula for success to? As in any growing, large-scale operation, there are several obstacles. From the viewpoint of many people, a big turnout of thousands is a measure of success. But this sheer size introduces new challenges. How does one manage a congregation of thousands? What does the church do to make sure the masses are not turned off by the size? How does the church deliver a spiritual message to a large group without making it sound like a canned piece of techno nonsense? Furthermore, how does the church adapt to the changing demographic of the unchurched and attract new people?

One of the first things the Warren ministry looked at was changing what the church looked like. It had to simultaneously not look like the traditional white-steeple churches of the past *and* be inviting to the unchurched. Saddleback accomplished that objective in a two-step process. The first was to set up a place of worship wherever the church could, if need be in a rented space other than a traditional church building. The second step was to build a church that was huge, but not crowded; could accommodate large groups, but have walkways and views that were private, serene, and spiritual. Saddleback Valley Community Church accomplished that objective.

The current challenges involve looking at the facility of today and seeing the facility of tomorrow. Today, Saddleback must budget and manage structures, utilities, parking facilities, and landscaping. This can be potentially problematic if the budgets get too large or if the maintenance becomes a distraction from the mission of Saddleback. So everything is done to make sure that the facility and physical operations of Saddleback don't get in the way of evangelizing the unchurched. At the same time, these physical operations must stay true to the mission of making the unchurched feel spiritually welcome.

In the future, Saddleback must think about how to expand its operations while staying on course. What happens when the current property—as large as it is—suddenly starts to feel crowded? Are more services offered at different times of the day? Does the facility need to annex more property and build again? Or does Saddleback have to establish branch locations in the area? The bigger question may be "Where and how does the next generation want to worship?"

This leads to the next challenge: who are the unchurched today and who will be the unchurched of the next generation? The church must approach these people on two fronts, as it did in the beginning: knock down the barriers that keep the unchurched away, and provide an atmosphere that brings them in.

In knocking down the barriers, the biggest challenge facing the mega churches is their image. Regardless of their intent, or even their results, mega churches have a negative image among the newest generation of worshipers. Mega churches by name sound corporate, structured, and very impersonal. They represent an older generation that flies Southwest Airlines and shops at Wal-Mart. Regardless of how customer service–conscious these entities are—and they certainly are—their image to the next generation is a negative one.

So how does a Church Growth Movement mega church battle this image effectively? Make no mistake about it, there are ministries and groups at Saddleback already gathering and working on this challenge. Will there be more, smaller church settings? Will there be a church that has *more* images and signs of Christianity instead of less? Are there focus groups and individual ministries that are currently engaging the current unchurched as well as the next generation of worshipers? These are all of the questions that Rick Warren is continually asking his congregation to answer as he continues on his mission to evangelize the unchurched.

One answer to the image problem may be found in Rick's own advice to smaller churches. Through the pastoral seminars hosted at Saddleback as well as the information-rich Pastor.com website, Rick provides guidance and tools for small churches to successfully evangelize. From a marketing perspective, he advises the pastors to look at three concepts:

1. Understand what motivates your church.

2. Have a clear destination.

3. Reach out to the community.

Taking each of these individually sheds more light on how this—and ultimately Rick Warren's ministry—can succeed for the small church.

Understand what motivates your church. Why do people come to church? What is their purpose? Churches often fall into the rut of routine. After a while, people are attending church as a task, not as a spiritually fulfilling event. The sermons are the same, the delivery is the same, the church itself never changes—except for the occasional fresh coat of white paint—and the congregation stays the same, never gathering new members.

By falling into a routine, churches forget the mission: evangelize. They can only evangelize if they are willing to bring in new people. In order to grow, the church has to be constantly challenging itself to change its physical, spiritual, and congregational makeup.

Have a clear destination. By delineating five purposes for his church (membership, maturity, ministry, mission, and magnification), Warren ensures that his Saddleback congregants have a clear set of objectives to pursue in their spiritual lives. This weaves the purposes into every aspect of church life. Programs such as CLASS are an important part of defining the destination clearly. Warren encourages other pastors to take his approaches and modify them to accommodate their religious community's needs.

"Build it and they will come" does not work. There has to be a significant amount of community outreach to find and attract the unchurched. *Reach out to the community* is the third concept. The best church can be built in the best location, but it's just like fishing. The fisherman can make a great cast to a great spot. He may know it and his friends may know it, but it only matters if the fish know it. The church must take action to reach out to the community. Also, it must define its role in the surrounding area before the area can define it for the church.

Rick Warren says that there's no secret to church growth. The greatest lesson he has learned is to develop a formula and then continually improve on it. Other churches need to follow this fundamental concept, but tailor it specifically for their needs. They must be aware that whatever works today may not very well work tomorrow. For some young parishes, that will mean staying away from the model of mega churches. For others, it will mean striving to reach the same epic size as Saddleback—or even larger. Warren believes that the only standard that should apply to all Christian churches is a commitment to God's mission.

Ripple Effects: Creating Leaders

At the center of Rick Warren's theory of church growth is the pastor. Rick has always understood that pastors are the agents of constructive change in the religious community and the world. Pastors, not church politics, are the solution to the problems in the Christian community and, in a larger sense, the world community.

Warren has geared a significant number of his Saddleback seminars and programs toward pastors and church leaders. The pastor-to-pastor connection is the driving force behind his low-profile, yet highly active, approach to spreading the lessons learned at Saddleback. He prefers this approach and considers it more effective than the higher-profile, over-the-top television approach.

What are the results? Rick Warren's website, Pastor.com, has had feedback that more than 180,000 pastors have implemented some of his ideas at their own churches. People from all fifty states and thirty foreign countries have attended the Purpose-Driven Ministries conference held at Saddelback, including 3,800 for the May 2002 conference. Many of these churches report an increase in church enrollment of at least 30 percent, while others report significantly higher increases.

Rick sometimes expresses concern that many young pastors aren't getting the kind of education they need in order to live up to their hefty responsibility. Church poll-taker George Barna echoes, "Our seminaries don't train leaders. Churches are crying out for strong, visionary, Godly leadership." He fears that church positions are being filled by teachers who are good people, but not true Christian leaders committed to creating a collective vision for their congregation.

Adding to this comment, Rick talks about churches losing their sense of purpose. Churchgoers fall into the routine of saying prayers, giving to charity, and taking communion without really backing it up with the feeling of true worship and commitment to God. That sort of superficial church participation is exactly what he's trying to fight in *The Purpose-Driven Life.*

Reflections on Warren

It's not an exaggeration to say that Rick Warren and his Saddleback ministry have influenced millions of people around the world. His pastor-oriented seminars and conferences have received significant acclaim and continue to grow. The popularity of *The Purpose-Driven Life* and the forty-day program is an example of Rick's universal success.

What's remarkable is that in spite of all his accomplishments, Rick has never become complacent. He continues to work tirelessly to expand and develop this dynamic ministry, pushing the envelope of Christian evangelism. A never-ending thirst to reach out to those on the fringes of society keeps his fires of purpose burning. His programs help alcoholics, drug abusers, prisoners, and other disenchanted men and women seeking the meaning of life. His training seminars have helped Catholics, Jews, Muslims, Methodists, and Mormons. His is truly a ministry that moves across barriers.

Perhaps most remarkable is the way that Rick has managed to spread his message while avoiding the corrupting influences of fame and fortune. The fact that the Saddleback ministry—whose leader rarely makes appearances outside of his own church—has asserted itself so extensively in the world is a testament to the power and effectiveness of Rick Warren's plan.

Rick Warren is, without a doubt, one of the most charismatic and successful Christian leaders in the modern world. His theories and methods for church growth have had unprecedented effects in the Christian community. He would also be the first to say that these ideas are not his own. In his mind, only God can make the church grow. He'll admit that dynamic, inspiring pastors are necessary components of church growth—but only as far as they help do the work God sets forth. As Rick says, "It's not about you".

Warren understands that we are living in troubled times filled with confusing doctrines, volatile political movements, economic hardships, and war. He also understands that people of all backgrounds, races, and religions are searching for guidance. They are seekers. In the face of hardship people come to realize their true purpose in life: to serve God.